Learn to Pain

WILDLIFE

Martin Knowelden

COLLINS

First published in 1985
by William Collins Sons & Co., Ltd
London · Glasgow · Sydney
Auckland · Toronto · Johannesburg

New edition 1986

© Ruan Martin Ltd 1985, 1986

Design and photography by Rupert Brown
Filmset by Media Conversion Limited
Colour reproduction by Positive Colour

ISBN 0 00 412125 2

Printed and bound in Italy
by New Interlitho SpA, Milan

CONTENTS

PORTRAIT OF AN ARTIST
MARTIN KNOWELDEN

Martin Knowelden was born in 1943 in Borehamwood, Hertfordshire, which was at that time still a rural community.

He cannot remember a time when he was not interested in drawing and painting wildlife – his mother still has a drawing of a mouse that he did when he was two. Animals featured in everything he did at primary school, even in a poster to advertise the school sports day that was set as a class project. As a junior schoolboy, Martin kept a menagerie of small creatures – newts, slow-worms, grass snakes, frogs, sticklebacks and mice – all caught locally. With school friends, some of whom came from neighbouring farms, he also learnt to hunt, often with ferrets, and to rear small birds of prey.

The young Knowelden's reputation as a 'mender of sick and lame birds' led to a succession of unusual house guests, the most notable being a jackdaw called Duncan which was hand-reared and lived free in the garden when not perching on Martin's head as he cycled to and from school.

It was at Borehamwood Grammar School that Martin was first introduced to pottery, carving, sculpture, the history of art and, in particular, the philosophy of Gustave Courbet. Later, in 1960, he was accepted at the Art School attached to Watford Technical College where he attained his National Diploma in Design (NDD).

After his first job with a local advertising agency he joined the TV Graphics department of the BBC. Two years later he returned to Borehamwood with a job at ATV (now Central Television) where he specialized in animation and programme graphics.

During these years Martin felt that both Borehamwood and he had lost touch with their rural beginnings, and in 1971 he formed a design and illustration partnership with designer Rupert Brown, setting up a studio on the banks of the River Stour in Suffolk. They undertook a wide range of work and the discipline of having to draw a hydraulic piston with an airbrush one day, followed by a cutaway of a medieval church the next, is something Martin considers the most useful experience for any artist.

His involvement with wildlife publications stemmed from his first one-man show of paintings and drawings. A publisher asked him to illustrate a book on rats, and this led to a wide variety of book illustration.

Martin draws a clear distinction between illustrating (for books, magazines and advertising) and painting. He has had exhibitions of paintings, drawings and bronzes in Europe and North America as well as in the UK, most recently at the Tryon gallery, London. He is currently working his way through a series of commissioned works in oil, with subjects including salmon fishing on the Wye, Jack Russell terriers hunting, and golden eagles in Wester Ross. These commissions are sandwiched between a series of paintings for six children's books and a book on hunting birds.

Martin now lives in the village of West Wratting, Cambridgeshire, with his wife and their two children. He grows all his own vegetables and greatly enjoys cooking and winemaking. He loves poetry and jazz and follows a wide variety of country sports. He breeds lurchers, keeps ferrets, and is an experienced falconer.

With scrupulous attention to detail Martin Knowelden offers in his wildlife paintings a very personal view which combines quite opposing elements. His treatment of animals in their natural habitat is sometimes hard and always unromantic, often revealing the harshness of life in the wild. The beauty of nature is always clearly present, however, and his work shows a sincere respect born out of his knowledge of this world. He quite obviously delights in the minutiae of his subjects, sometimes taking an almost microscopic view and delineating every pore and whisker. He has an unfailing eye for the unusual pose or situation, the incongruous prop and the intriguing composition, and includes in his paintings a wealth of subtle details, some of them decidedly tongue-in-cheek, to intrigue and puzzle the viewer. His work not only shows quite clearly his love, and his knowledge, of his subject, but also his love of paint. The play of light and shade, and the visual effects created by water are two recurring themes among many which demonstrate his genuine delight in capturing his quarry as a highly original image on paper or canvas.

Fig. 1 Martin Knowelden at work in his studio

SELF-PORTRAIT

I cannot recall a time in my life when I was not drawing animals and birds. Growing up in a little Hertfordshire village which was beginning to expand with London's overspill, I, and my friends, resorted to the countryside at every opportunity for our recreation. We knew where to go to watch badgers and the ways of foxes. We tracked roebuck and rabbits and kept mice and slow-worms in our bedrooms. I helped the injured and sick wildlife of all kinds and made ready use of the opportunity it afforded for close and careful study. I thought the first kestrel I reared and trained the most exquisite thing in creation and I have re-expressed that feeling with all the wild creatures I have ever come close to.

Much of the time that I was not actively abroad in the countryside, I was at home with pencils and paints, trying to draw it, and the animals that lived in it. I was continually frustrated by an inability to achieve on paper the beauty and vitality of the creatures I saw in the wild and, eventually, I found myself studying the wildlife about me with the express purpose of drawing and painting it more perfectly. The number of the halt and the lame (mostly birds) I collected increased and a rather gruesome collection of bones, teeth, wings and claws began, to which I am still adding today. Although I did not appreciate it at the time, and simply studied and drew nature because it was an enjoyable preoccupation, I realize now the distinct correlation between observation and the quality of my drawings. It is true for all artists, whether professional or amateur, that the best of their work will be that which is most carefully and sympathetically observed.

I am still frustrated by the gulf between my paintings and the reality, but we learn from each picture done and, hopefully, improve as we learn. While I know that perfection is unobtainable, striving for it remains exciting and inspiring.

Not only does the desire to paint animals demand study and research, but the techniques of using paints and brushes, pencils and paper, watercolour and washes need practising and perfecting. There are so many permutations and possibilities to explore, and each one of us must find the most successful, the most suitable for himself. Developing a style and applying it to a particular subject like wildlife can be the most satisfying of achievements.

I must leave research and study for each of you to work out for yourself. Circumstances, opportunity and commitment will decide for you the amount you need to do, but the techniques and the tools, the order in which things are best done, and the rules and guidelines within which your work will be achieved are much the same for all of us, and I can describe those which I have found most useful in the hope that they form a base on which anyone can build a style of their own. Let us now consider a general approach to wildlife painting.

I have always delighted in the machinery of painting. The textures of watercolour paper, the shapes of palette knives and scrapers, the brilliance of a new canvas – the list goes on. Equipment becomes worn and polished with time and patinated by paint and spirit, and familiar tools fit the hand comfortably, becoming irreplaceable allies in the business of making pictures. Get to know your equipment in this way. Enjoy using your tools and practise until you no longer need to think about them but can work automatically, the brush or pencil becoming an extension of your hand. You can then give your whole

attention to the painting itself. The worth of a wildlife picture is in the quality the artist imparts to his subject which makes it not merely a representation of a creature in the wild, as is a photograph, but suggests the character and nature of that creature, and makes the viewer aware of the intangibles. A good picture shows, within its forms and composition, the grace, the power, the intelligence: abstracts which can never be delineated, yet are clearly there in the 'mood' of the piece. It should contain the essence of its subject, make a definitive statement. With these problems to ponder, as you work at your canvas, you do not want to have to worry about which way up the brush goes!

What I have tried to do in this book is describe, from my own experience, the practices involved in gathering together all the separate threads that finally make up the finished work. Starting with field notes and sketching, through studio drawings and studies, and finally composing and executing your picture, the procedures described here are all those I use myself and which resulted in all the pictures in this book.

Some techniques will come easily and others will most certainly not. Do not spend a lot of time, all at once, on those which prove difficult but, rather, work on them a little each time you sit down to paint. Remember that art is only 1 per cent inspiration and 99 per cent perspiration, so work – observation and practice – is the major requirement. Your skills will never develop without it. The more precision and careful study that you get into your preparations for a painting, the more depth you will impart to it. Finally, and above all, never let anything you do become a chore. There is no value whatsoever in a picture or a drawing that is finished reluctantly. Let all your work be, as mine is, the product of enjoyment and pleasure, and an abiding fascination in your subject.

Fig. 2 Martin Knowelden with his ferruginous hawk

WHY PAINT WILDLIFE?

The first images ever made by man were of wild animals. Captured in exquisite economy, using pigments on the smooth walls of caves, are scenes depicting our earliest ancestors and dotted with creatures recognizable still as zebra, buffalo, giraffe and all kinds of antelope. Men with spears, bows and clubs, accompanied by curly-tailed dogs, weave in and out of these panoramic murals. Why these images were created we can never know with certainty, yet, even before man had formalized his gods, he was recording a relationship with the wild creatures of his environment in colour and line. Since these earliest records, man's attitudes to animals have been complex and contradictory. Some suggest that these early paintings were inspired by a mystical belief that the capture of an animal's image was analogous to the capture of the beast itself. The qualities of wild creatures – the cat, the hawk, the jackal, the ram, the scarab beetle and the serpent – were apportioned to the deities of ancient Egypt, and their depiction as man-bodied and animal-headed reflects the complex interaction of man and nature as perceived by the artists and sculptors of that long-dead civilization.

Many primitive societies carved and painted the symbols of their worship in animal forms, and this 'totemism' is evident in the wealth of animal representation seen all around us today. The beasts of the primitive totem makers have their modern-day counterparts in the lion at Britannia's side and the American eagle, both symbols of strength, reliability and courage we all recognize. Behind them is a vast array of creatures, each with its special qualities, symbolizing all aspects of our own lives and embodying ideals that we might all aspire to. The symbols of trade and industry featuring animals are legion and there are countless examples ranging from these to the tattooist's art, with every conceivable sphere in between.

The Victorians' sentimentality saw in animal behaviour lessons and moral pointers for us all to heed; Aesop had shown this with considerable humour, and much more vigour, centuries earlier. Yet Gustave Courbet, the French painter who became the father of modern art, derived from his hunter's knowledge of wildlife, combined with his careful study of animal life as an artist, a clearer understanding of his own place in the great scheme of creation.

Whatever the reasons for attempting the painting of wildlife (and I suppose there are as many reasons as there are people wishing to try it), let us begin with the simplest of motivations, the easiest to understand: admiration. For example, one sees a simple admiration for such creatures, so at one with their environment, in the cave paintings at Lascaux, and I look for no deeper or more obscure reason for their creation. Whilst they may be much more, they are certainly a celebration of superior strength and speed; skills in coping with hunger, drought and weather; abilities for providing shelter and food for their young; and, above all, freedom under the sky. Wild animals have always fascinated and intrigued us and, for some of us, this fascination has manifested itself in a desire to capture, as did our ancestors, some essence, some definitive quality stated in colour and line. The act of painting a mammal, bird or fish in a way which sums up some fundamental quality of character is, in itself, an expression of admiration, and if the image so made imparts that feeling to those who see it after, the work is properly one of art.

At its very best, animal art makes a profound statement about man's relationship to the rest of creation. At its most humble, the artist simply uses the many beautiful colours and the myriad remarkable forms that nature provides as the basis, the foundation, on which rests his own desire to create.

Whatever the motivation, taking a sketchbook and field glasses into the countryside and collecting material for use in the studio, as well as the general study of nature with the painted image in mind, is an absorbing and satisfying pastime. With sufficient practice to achieve a commercial standard and with an understanding of the demand from so many areas for animal and natural-history imagery, there is no reason why your hobby should not also be a source of income.

Backgrounds

The way we see wildlife, as a general rule, is in brief, sudden glimpses. Human eyes are so placed that we have a field of focused vision of about 17 degrees and we scan our surroundings either by moving the eyes themselves or by utilizing the articulation of the head. When we suddenly catch sight of a wild creature, we tend to fix on the animal (and on its eyes in particular if possible), and everything outside that 17-degree field is perceived as blurred vision, unfocused and indistinct. The animal becomes a vivid, sharply defined object on a vague, soft background, like a sparkling gemstone on a velvet tray.

Backgrounds, then, seem to be seen as impressions and, for the purposes of impact in your picture, they are, with some notable exceptions, best kept less than sharp. Aim for bold colour and strong lines that lead the eye to the focal point of the picture plane, without distracting it with unnecessary detail. An equal degree of finish over the whole painting gives the eye no 'high point' to fix on, no contrast or conflict to resolve, and consequently the picture lacks power.

I always start an oil painting by deciding on an overall general colour, usually dark green or dark brown, and laying it over the whole picture area, whether paper, canvas or board, with a wide flat brush, say a Dalon D.88 ½ inch (or 1 inch for larger pictures). I let the natural texture that the brush imparts form the basis for the background. Grass and rock require quite different surface textures, yet I form both by the same technique – rubbing or scraping away the dark base colour to reveal the pale surface colour beneath. Experiment with this 'drawing in reverse' technique on scraps of paper or canvas; it can be very effective. I begin painting highlights into this base, developing and detailing the most the areas nearest the subject of the picture. I then mix a very dark colour (enough to last, for it will be needed for shading over the whole work), which is sympathetic with the base colour, perhaps the same dark green or brown I began with, and add it as shadow, rounding out and giving depth to the forms delineated earlier.

Backgrounds are as varied as subjects and need a varied approach. Some subjects might require no more than a colour wash or 'tint' to offset the focus, while another might well demand a complex tracery of leaves, flowers, branches and grass. There are no hard and fast rules and you must decide for yourself just how far, or in what direction, you must go according to the particular piece you wish to work on, or your particular style. There are one or two basic pointers, however, well worth bearing in mind. The background of a painting functions as the setting for a jewel; the gold surround supporting a diamond. It must enhance and underline the beauty of the centre of focus; it must frame and isolate; it should lend importance, making the viewer aware that the subject deserves special attention.

Once you have a clear mental picture of how you wish your finished piece to appear, you should establish just how 'finished', how detailed and polished, your subject will turn out. The background should then be worked backwards, as it were, from this point, never competing with the subject by equalling its 'finish', yet complementing and encouraging it, making the total of the work more than the sum of the parts. Remember that cold colours – blues, greens and tints based on the blue end of the spectrum – recede; they seem to go back into the canvas as you look at it. Warm colours project; reds and browns and the tints from the spectrum's yellow end seem to come towards you as you view the canvas. Use this optical effect for your own ends: a fox hidden in the grass would appear much more hidden in brown or yellow grass than in spring grass, lush and green. The colour of the fox, being a warm colour, projects out of the canvas and the colour of the grass can either throw it into sharp relief (if it is green and therefore recedes) or can complement and soften the subject (if it is yellow or brown and projects with the subject).

Shadow can be used to increase depth, anchor an object to a surface, or describe or reinforce the form of a subject by the line it takes as it falls across your scene. It can also be used to emphasize the texture of a background and is, of course, a simple way of justifying a dark or black background for anything pale or white which needs a clearly defined edge.

WHAT EQUIPMENT DO YOU NEED?

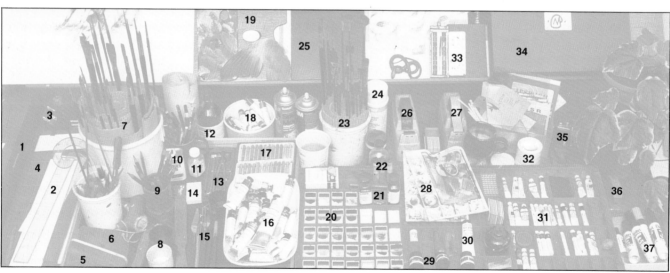

Fig. 3

Key to materials

1	Metre straightedge	8	Dipping pots	18	Gouache paints	28	Watercolour palettes
2	Perspex rule	9	Pencils	19	Oil palettes	29	Drawing inks
3	Mount cutter	10	Lighter fuel	20	Watercolour pans	30	Gel retarder
4	Cutting mat	11	Masking fluid	21	Varnishes	31	Watercolour tube paints
5	Desk brush	12	Linseed oil	22	Rotring inks	32	Paint wells
6	Emery cloth	13	Rotring compass	23	Watercolour brushes	33	Portable watercolour box
7	Brushes (Dalon) for oils	14	Putty rubber	24	Aerosol fixative	34	Portable oil painting set
		15	Palette knives	25	Sketchbook	35	35mm SLR camera
		16	Oil paints	26	Sellotape	36	Stapler
		17	Pastels	27	Draughting tape	37	Felt tip pens

Modern paints – oils, watercolour and gouache – are of superb quality, and while they may appear expensive as you survey the price list, a little goes a long way and they are, with proper use, very good value. A reputable supplier, like George Rowney, offers a huge range of pigments in several sizes and qualities, catering for amateur, student and professional artists.

Oils

Start with a comprehensive range of basic colours and wait until you have practised your palette for a while before you buy any of the more exotic colours. I would suggest you start with the primaries – blue, yellow and red – in two forms, 'hard' and 'soft'. I would describe Prussian Blue, Rowney Golden Yellow and Cadmium Scarlet as 'soft' primaries. Mixed with Zinc White (a 'transparent' white), they produce tints which are mellow and organic. Coeruleum, Lemon Yellow and Rose Doré are 'hard' primaries. Derived, as most 'hard' colours are, from mineral or chemical pigments, they throw tints which are hard, clean and brilliant. These six colours should form the basic colour box to satisfy any requirement; simply add to these black and white.

It is as well here to describe the three whites. Flake White is a lead-based paint and, consequently, is dangerous if misused. It matures with a warm, amber tinge and is reasonably permanent, giving mellow tints and a 'glow' to work as it ages. It covers well used neat. (Permanence is the ability a colour has to remain as painted. Some violets and maroons change their colour very rapidly if left exposed to light; such colours are the opposite of permanent, i.e. fugitive.) Titanium White is derived from a mineral pigment and is brilliant and hard, giving off a lot of light. It, too, is permanent, although not to the same degree as Flake, and mixes a clean, sharp tint. Zinc White is produced with zinc oxide and is the least solid of the three. It is just as permanent as the others but imparts a translucent quality to its tints and can be used for building up layers of colour. Choose whichever white you feel most suitable (or buy one of each) and, with Lamp Black, your basic colour box is complete. I would, however, suggest that you add the earth colours – Vandyke Brown, Raw Sienna, and Yellow Ochre – and a good base green with very high permanence is Terre Verte.

There are about ninety colours in Rowney's Artists' range and about sixty in the Georgian range, so you can accumulate a completely comprehensive set of pigments as you progress and establish exactly which colours are suited to your requirements. For the amateur, the Georgian range is one of excellent quality at a very reasonable price.

You will also need a spirit in order to dilute your colour and an oil for your basic medium. Use turpentine for your diluent, and for your medium, linseed oil is unbeatable. For outdoor work or sketching,

Rowney's Gel Medium or Alkyd Medium mixed with oil paints are really excellent and dry in half the time oils take. Copal Varnish is a useful addition to your equipment, too. Thinned with turps, it can be used to varnish a finished work and, mixed with turps and linseed oil, it forms a beautifully smooth medium with oil colour, allowing easier brushing and a faster rate of drying. If you intend to get outdoors with your paints, and you are starting from scratch, you could do no better than to get one of Rowney's ready-fitted boxes. The 'Weybridge' gives you charcoal, a palette knife, dippers, brushes, linseed oil, turpentine, twelve tubes of colour with an extra white, and a good, firm palette. The box is robust and well made, just the right size, with a handle, and is excellent value.

Watercolours and gouache

The difference between watercolour and gouache is in the nature of the paint itself. Watercolour gives a clean and transparent tint which is used as a thin wash on damped paper. The colour of the paper shows through and gives watercolour its luminous or glowing quality. Gouache is an opaque or solid pigment which is thinned with water and used on textured card or board, much as oil paint.

Both forms of paint can be bought in tubes, either individually or in sets, and watercolour also comes in blocks known as pans. I prefer pans as they are long-lasting and easy to keep clean. There are about sixty watercolours in Rowney's Artists' range and about thirty in the Georgian range, but to start with you will only need a selection of basic colours similar to those listed above for oils. Rowney's WT10WB watercolour box includes an excellent range of ten tubes, two brushes (one for washes) and a china palette. The HP22WB is the same well-made box, with the same brushes and china palette but pans instead of tubes. Rowney's Designers' Gouache in 22-ml tubes is excellent and their introductory trial set is great value. Their Acrylising Medium makes gouache water-resistant and allows clean overpainting of colours without 'pick-up'.

Brushes

Brushes, for me, are no longer the problem they were, thanks to Dalon. The synthetic fibre used for these brushes is incredibly fine and ideal for oils; I use, now, nothing else. Even in the smallest sizes they are, in my opinion, the equal of any natural-hair brush and, what is more, they stand up even to my careless and heavy-handed treatment. (They come back to new with an occasional application of paint-stripper!) I have brushes from the whole range and I will pass on a useful tip here: get into the routine of buying one or two brushes each week (Dalons are incredibly good value) and work your brushes in over a period. I try to avoid using a pot of brushes until they all need retiring and then having to start again with a brand-new set. It is also a painless way of renewing your most important item of equipment.

There is, of course, a great range of brushes and you must try several before you find the one ideally suited to your needs. I have found the perfect brush, for myself, in the Dalon range and look no further – you will find your own in time.

Watercolour, however, can only be worked with brushes made of natural hair, and very fine hair at that. Sable is incredibly strong and springy, considering the fine nature of the hair, and comes from a mink-like creature from Eastern Europe and China. Sable is extremely expensive and works quite beautifully, and a watercolour brush, carefully cleaned and shaped after use, will last for years. The less commonly used sizes and the big ones used for washes of flat colour are made in less expensive mixtures of hair without any loss of quality. I use pure sable, ox and sable mix, and some squirrel. Watercolours are notoriously difficult to control with inferior brushes, so make life easy on yourself and buy one or two top-quality sables.

Always clean your brushes thoroughly with a clean rag and whatever solvent is relevant: turpentine with oils, water with gouache or watercolour. While still damp, smooth and shape the brush, then stand it, bristles upward, to dry out naturally. A coil of corrugated cardboard held inside an old coffee tin makes an excellent brush stand, the handles of the brushes being pushed into the corrugations.

Pencils

Pencils, although the most commonplace of all an artist's tools, cause confusion and discontent. A pencil is a wooden sleeve surrounding a core of graphite mixed with clay. The wooden surround is cut away with a knife to expose the graphite core, which gives a black line. The more clay you mix with your graphite, the harder the core (or 'lead') and, consequently, the finer and paler the drawn line. The less clay in the mixture, the softer and blacker the line; simple, really. The hardness of a pencil is graded in degrees of H, the softness in degrees of B; an HB pencil is the average of the two. Buy hexagonal (easier on the hand) drawing pencils of the best quality only (buy cheaply, buy twice), like Rowney's Victoria, in degrees HB, 2B and 6B. Shape your pencil point with a very sharp knife or one-sided razor blade to a long narrow point, the exposed lead being about a third of the overall sharpened tip. This allows you to use the sides of the pencil lead as well as the point. You will find a Black Beauty (an extra-fat 4B) very useful for filling in, and I prefer charcoal pencils to the traditional charcoal sticks. Kneadable putty rubbers are useful for more than just erasing. They can be used as one would use white to draw into a sketch, or as a burnisher to smooth and soften pencil lines. All pencil, conté (a densely black wax crayon) or charcoal

work needs fixing when finished to prevent smudging and you can choose a clear plastic varnish in an aerosol can or in a bottle with the old blow-pipe system.

Pens

Pens are a matter of personal preference. I do not like plastic pen holders as they are too short and too light (and plastic!), so I make bamboo holders of my own. I like the weight and feel of the wood and bamboo is non-tapering. I use sections of bamboo 10 mm ($\frac{3}{8}$ in) in diameter and 165 mm (6 $\frac{1}{2}$ in) long. Gillott nibs are unbeatable and practice will indicate which grade suits you best. Rowney produce an abundance of quality art materials and their 'Kandahar' drawing inks are among the best. They make a superb Sepia and their Black Indian is excellent, flowing like satin. I use only the black and the brown but there is a range of twenty colours including white.

Useful extras

You will find a number of odd tools very useful as you continue painting. A small, flexible palette knife, used to bring oil colours in from the edge of the palette to the centre for mixing, will keep colours clean and separate. A few scrapers for working into wet paint can either be made or found about the house. I have some sharpened bamboo, some old paintbrush handles with glued-in tips of bone and antler, and a variety of recycled knitting needles, chopsticks and screwdrivers. Broken combs make lovely patterns drawn across the canvas, and old toothbrushes make good stipplers. All I can say about these gadgets is that you will know one when you see it.

A maul-stick (the traditional artist's stick with a padded end) will keep your sleeves off your canvas when you work, will give you a straight edge for ruling brush lines or establishing horizontals and verticals, and will support your wrist for very small detail or precision work. To make one, use a metre (1 yd) length of 7 mm ($\frac{1}{4}$ in) copper tubing (any DIY shop has it) and bind on a chamois-leather pad at one end. Other useful aids are a pair of dividers, which will save you time and effort when transferring proportions on to the canvas, and, of course, compasses – very few people can draw a perfect circle freehand.

Save the plastic caps from aerosol cans; they make perfect dippers and you can discard any that become too encrusted. Rags are essential and must be free of any fluff which might transfer to your paint surface.

Painting surfaces

And now the problem of what to paint on. Watercolour papers are many and varied, giving more or less surface, greater or lesser strength, different degrees of absorption, and a wide range of textures. The prices vary considerably according to the structure of the material (paper is made from many dif-

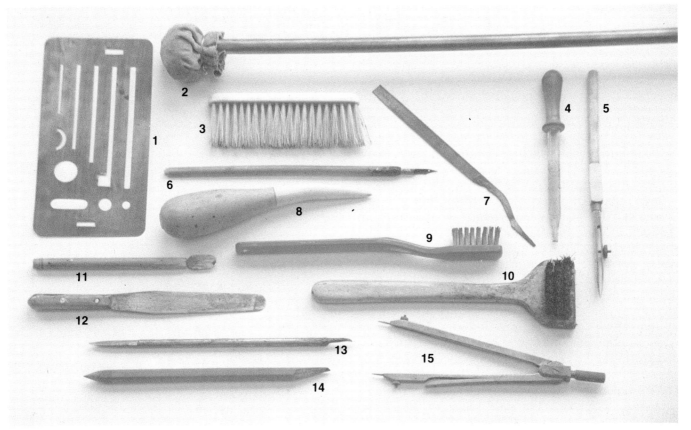

Fig. 4

1 Masking template	6 Cane-handled mapping pen	13 Brass scraper
2 Maul-stick	7 Saw-toothed scraper	14 Bamboo scraper
3 Small cleaning brush	8 Burnisher	15 Dividers
4 Dropper	9 & 10 Brush stipplers	
5 Ruling pen	11 & 12 Mini palette knives	

ferent fibre types, rag being one of the best, wood pulp one of the coarsest) and the method of production (some are still hand-made). Once again the rule must be to try them and find out for yourself which is most suitable for your own purposes; but, to start with, you will find Bockingford 150 gm² as good as any. It has a smooth grain, suitable for drawing, and enough surface, or 'nap', for watercolour. An A2 pad is probably the easiest way to buy it.

For oils you have a choice of grains from rough to smooth, in canvas either ready-mounted on a stretcher or off the roll. Rough-grained is probably best left until you are well practised. Gesso is a very fine plaster and size mixture, resembling double cream, which, used as a primer on your canvas, produces a surface as fine and smooth as paper. You can buy canvas, ready-primed, mounted on thick card squares, which are especially handy for outdoors or sketching. Gesso can also be used to prime hardboard or heavy cardboard, both popular and economical surfaces and both good for wildlife subjects because they are smooth and texture-free. There are many papers specially prepared for oil-paint sketching and you should buy a good block, say thirty sheets, A2 size, preferably with a waterproof jacket. For sketching or finished work, Rowney's oil painting paper or Daler's Tyneham paper are ideal.

A drawing board is an excellent basic work-top and is easily carried with your paper in a sketching bag. It can be propped up on a table or used with an easel for painting indoors. Buy a wooden board, about 65 × 45 cm (25 ½ × 17 ¾ in). Easels come in a wide range of types and prices and you should choose the best you can afford for the space you have available. If you want an outdoor one, a lightweight wooden sketching easel with collapsible legs and a carrying handle is ideal. For indoors, something more solid is better.

All this is still only the basic equipment, and one of the great pleasures of painting is the accumulation of materials and tools. You will want, as time goes by, much which I have not mentioned here, and a good relationship with your local art shop will prove invaluable. There are doubtless many items I would never think of using, which you will come to regard as irreplaceable in your paintbox.

Finally, take care when storing pictures. Watercolours should be kept out of the light, in a drawer, say, laid flat and protected by a sheet of tissue. Oils need to be stored upright and, when dry (sometimes this can take six months), varnished with a proprietary picture varnish of the brush-on or aerosol type.

TECHNIQUES

An artist's style – that which makes one person's work quite distinct from any other's – comes about because of the unique way in which each individual uses his or her tools. Van Gogh's short, stabbing, flat brush strokes, flowing in coils, or Seurat's tiny points of colour, mixing on the canvas, are both immediately recognizable. You must experiment and practise with the tools at your disposal and find out the range and versatility of each one; what each piece of equipment can do for you. I have a small Rowney watercolour box which is invaluable for field notes and yet contains only eighteen quarter pans and one No. 4 round-end sable. These, I soon discovered, are sufficient for all the jobs I need doing out-of-doors, from colour washes to fine pen lines. A 5mm HB automatic pencil completes the kit, and I keep them all in a sketching satchel hanging, always ready, by the studio door.

You have only to look through an art supplier's catalogue to realize the vast range of tools and materials at your disposal. Experiment with as much as you can and try to reduce your requirements to a good, comprehensive, basic toolbox. Discover what serves your needs best and concentrate your practice on those techniques exclusively until they are second nature. When you are thoroughly conversant with your medium, like a musician who has mastered his scales, you can go on to improvise constructively.

The main tools of the artist are pencils and brushes, and the effects they can produce deserve some study. It is worth remembering that, artist or bricklayer, you should let the tools do the work for you.

Brush effects

In the case of brushes, practice will soon show you that one good-quality sable will give you a wide 'vocabulary'; a great range of textures and lines. Fill your brush with black watercolour wash and draw it across the paper from left to right at varying speeds. If it drips or splutters or in any way behaves on its own, take note how and why. It may well be of use. As the brush dries, gently splay out the fibres and see what marks you can achieve now. Lay the brush flat on the paper and roll it along. Discover the effects that you can get with the point, side, and flat of the brush, using it wet and dry alternately. Practise guiding your brush in as many different ways as you can and build up a set of practice sheets for reference. When you feel you have done enough with watercolour, begin again with oil paint, using turpentine substitute to thin your pigment to a wash.

Fig. 5 Fox and vixen: rendering the fur effect with a brush

Any new equipment requires practice to get the best results. Try another simple exercise: take an A3 sheet of watercolour paper and pencil in a grid, five spaces by five, giving you twenty-five squares. Take your new brush (or pen or pencil) and try to achieve a different texture in each square. A brush can be pushed as well as drawn across the page, and the tips of the bristles will give you stippling while the flat side gives you dabs of colour. Try your brush full of paint, then again almost dry. Pin up this sheet of textures

Fig. 6 Flying duck: several different brush techniques combined to achieve texture and tonal value

where you can refer to it when you come to your finished work.

Without practice you will struggle to achieve effects that with the right tools used in the right way you will find simple and quick; anything in your painting that is laborious or has been tedious to achieve will look like it. Wildlife, more than any other subject, needs to be spontaneous and full of life.

The watercolour sketch of the duck (**fig. 6**) illustrates the use of several effects coming from one brush. The textures of plumage, beak, leg and eye were all created with a Dalon Series D.77 No. 8, using basically single-stroke work. The foxes (**fig. 5**), sketched after a farmer's shoot, were done with pen and ink, and I could well have spent hours rendering the fur had I tried to carry on with the pen. As it was, I used my No. 8 Dalon again and rendered the fur effect in a few seconds. It also gives a far more convincing portrayal of the texture of fox-fur than any other method might have produced.

Fig. 7 Fine pencil

Fig. 8 Broad pencil

Pencil and pen effects

Fine pencil The beauty of a fine pencil is in its ability to achieve texture and tone by a series of criss-cross lines or 'hatching'. For wildlife studies, this technique gives marvellous precision for detail work. Keep a fine point on your pencil and a light touch, and build up density, as you would with watercolour, with a series of layers.

Broad pencil Strong, bold lines and areas of tone or shadow can be 'hacked' with a broad, soft pencil without wasting a lot of time. Use a long, tapering point and get your pencil to do the work by using the side of the lead as well as the point. Use your fingers to rub and shape areas of shadow. Aim to capture the essence of your subject in a few quick lines.

Fig. 9 Fine pen

Fig. 10 Broad pen

Fine pen A fine pen is an unforgiving tool and demands practice to achieve worthwhile results. It is rarely used in my studio, but it gives an effect, like steel engraving, which is impossible to get any other way. The prime requirement for fine pen work is patience!

Broad pen Any amount of finish is possible with a big nib, from loose, sketchy impressionism to highly finished realism. Use your pen freely and quickly, seeing what effects the pen itself can make. Develop and adapt those which suit your style best. Doodling is great practice.

17

ANATOMY

Just as you must practise a range of basic techniques to get the results you want from your equipment, so you must familiarize yourself with your subjects to achieve any worthwhile images. All creatures, in their construction, obey certain strict rules. Movement and form are limited by these underlying rules and the artist must learn what goes on under the skin of the creatures he wishes to paint if he is to impart any authority to his work, or bring any fuller understanding of his subject to the viewer.

Under the general heading 'anatomy', the artist should remember four elements which apply to fish, birds and mammals equally: frame, form, texture and colour. Let us look at each in turn.

Frame: the rigid skeleton which dictates the basic shape of the creature. Bones cannot stretch or bend so they give each animal a set of related measurements which are unchanging. Articulation is the movement of bones, one with another, at the joints. The remarkable complexity of bones in a bird's neck means it can articulate its head through 180 degrees and look directly backwards. The much poorer articulation of a toad's head means it must move its whole body to face in a given direction.

Form: the muscles which clothe the skeleton and give the animal a range of postures. There are certain poses characteristic of each specific animal, and the

Fig. 11   The underlying structure of a squirrel's frame (tail not shown)

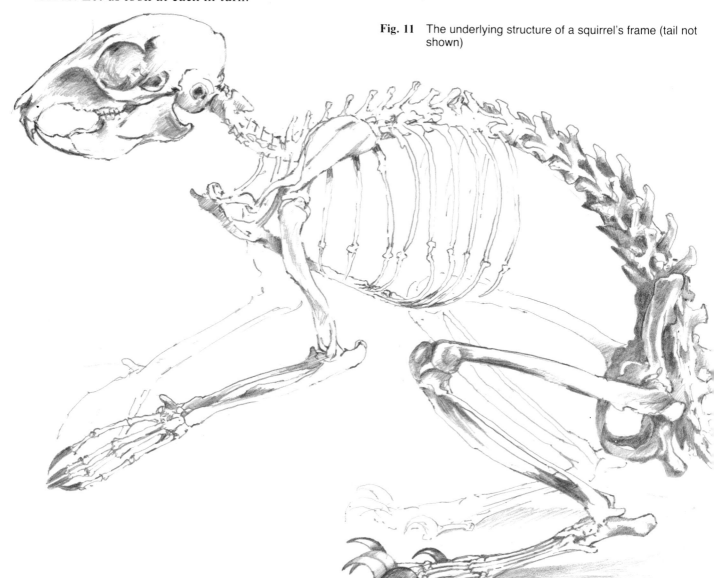

MAMMALS

changing shape of muscle describes activity or rest, anger or calm.

Texture: the 'feel' of the surface of your subject. Smooth fur, shaggy fur, smooth scales, rough prickles, wetness or dryness.

Colour: the artist must observe closely the colour of his subject. A white cat sitting in sunshine will carry gold and orange highlights and warm grey shading. In artificial light its colour will be hard white in illumination and a clean middle blue in shadow. Your subjects not only carry their intrinsic colour and pattern but take on the tints of reflected light from their surroundings.

The only way you will acquire the knowledge you need in the above categories is by studying, and a pencil and sketchbook should never be far away from you in case an opportunity for making notes or drawings comes along. If you have a dog or a cat, look carefully at how it is put together and how its tail, legs, ears, etc., join on to the trunk. Fish or fowl in the kitchen will give you a wealth of information as well as a good dinner!

Movement in an animal derives from its structure and should be most carefully portrayed. Until the camera caught horses in mid-gallop, it was normal for them to be painted with the forequarters stretched in front and the hindquarters stretched out at the back. This was later found to be quite incorrect. Stubbs had already realized from his very close study of anatomy (some of his drawings of horse musculature are still used in veterinary text-books, so accurate and complete are they) that horses, when galloping, move their legs in a rotary cycle which never allowed for the 'stretched' position conventionally painted. When Edouard Muybridge set up his long line of cameras to analyse movement more scientifically, his pictures of a galloping horse proved Stubbs to be right.

Perspective may shorten or stretch form, but must always convince the viewer that it is his viewpoint which causes these distortions and not the drawing of the subject itself which is inaccurate or wrong.

In conclusion, we have four main categories, plus movement and perspective which stem from them, to give us dependable guidelines when drawing or painting animals, and these are considered over the following twelve pages. Actual measurements are not essential, but relative sizes – that is, the proportions of one creature compared with another, or the size or weight of an animal's limbs in context with its body – are important. You must use your eyes!

The skeleton of the squirrel (**fig. 11**) is dominated by the backbone, which is massively built and exceptionally supple. It extends into the bones of the tail at the pelvis, and attaches to the skull at the atlas and axis vertebrae. This line from skull to tail tip describes the essential profile of the creature. The heavy bones of the hind legs articulate in such a way as to fold the legs away under the creature's body, leaving only the feet and toes showing. As the body moves there are key points where bones make changes on the skin surface. Knees, elbows, jaw-line, all the heavy black lines shown in **fig. 12**, are pressure points and dictate form for any given attitude the squirrel adopts. Drawing these charming animals in your local park will give you a wealth of positions and attitudes, but you will need a comprehensive knowledge of the underlying structures when you come to translate your sketches into a finished piece of work, where you may well wish to adapt and alter your preliminary drawings to get your composition exactly as you want it. The skeleton of the squirrel is fairly typical of the skeletons of most small mammals, so a working knowledge of it can be applied to other similar creatures.

Finally, if you reduce the skeleton to its major parts you will see that the head and ribcage can be drawn as two spheres, one (the head) two-thirds the size of the other. A connecting line runs from the head, over the top of the ribs, and on to the tail tip. Halfway down this line the hind legs can be drawn in as an S-shaped line and the fore legs are placed at the front end of the ribs. Drawing the long line of the backbone and tail will give you the posture: compressed for a crouching animal, flattened for the beast in flight, etc. The limbs and the bulk of the torso will always fit into place once this line has been established and, using field observation and your notebook, you will be able to place your subject in exactly the attitude you want.

Fig. 12 The points of mobility on the animal's surface

STUDYING YOUR SUBJECT

For anyone who walks regularly in the countryside, or in a local park, specimens from nature will often be found. Dead birds or mammals may seem unsavoury, but quick inspection (for the not too squeamish) will decide you as to their suitability for bringing back to your work-place for closer study. Natural specimens are invaluable for the wealth of detail they allow you to commit to paper. The process of drawing from life (or death in this case) has two prime functions: as you work carefully with pencil and paper, you are not only building your library of reference with an accumulating collection of drawings, you are fixing in your mind the detail which, taken as a whole, gives authenticity to your work. There is a third function also, less important perhaps but still contributing to the quality of your painting. As you move your specimen bird or mammal about, changing its position for sketching, you will begin to get a feeling of the creature's articulation: the way it moves. How far, for example, can a bird's wing stretch forward and then back? How do the toes of a mouse move from being wide-spread to closed? All these details – all this knowledge – are there in the background whenever you come to apply paint to paper or canvas.

As you get to know your subjects, you can set them up with pins or blocks in more lifelike positions. You will have to 'cheat' your drawing in many small ways so as to completely reinvest your subject with life. Incidentally, one word of warning about using an eraser. If you make a mistake and rub it out, you will almost certainly make the same mistake again. Leave all the lines in until you get the right one, then, if you must, erase carefully, reinforcing the correct line with pencil as you go. I prefer drawings with all the lines the artist makes intact. Augustus John's study of a whippet, with its vague profile made up of many exploratory lines, becomes not only a perfect work of reference, but so precisely captures the nervous tension of the dog as to elevate it to a true work of art.

Try pushing your model (I shall refer to whatever little corpses you may have collected as 'models' from now on) into a position where you have one side stretched and one side closed. In the case of the rat shown here, I positioned it in a typical pose using props and blocks and began a series of detailed drawings around one good general view of the complete animal. Sketch in with bold, simple lines the major areas of bulk in your model. Connect these with a profile (the line that you would draw if you were making a silhouette) which suggests tension. The hard, straight lines connecting curves suggest taut muscle, while depressed curves indicate slack. Now study your model for different textures. The sleek fur of the rat's back is shiny smooth, but the fluffy fur on the underparts appears dusty and diffused. Wet fur is spikey. With a brush, draw in a little of each. Now take a look at the detail of the rat's head. See how the fur there becomes finer in places until it disappears smoothly into the skin; see where follicles (the points on the skin where whiskers sprout) are placed. Study your own model and carefully draw in, with brush strokes which follow the direction of the hair, the contours around the small muscles of the face. These are crucial to animal painting as they give your subject facial expression. Make a special detail of the eye, opened wide, and note colour and size, for accuracy. Make details of the feet and fingers, and all the time you work, look at your model and then at your drawing for short, alternating periods. Draw a little, check a little, draw again, check again. Do not concentrate on one small area for too long at once, but jump from tail to ear, foot to eye, overall mass to detail of fingernail. Break off every few minutes, relax your concentration and look at something fresh for a few moments. Then go back to your drawing and your model with a new eye, and look at both for a while before starting to draw again. A discipline will develop which will be invaluable as a base for all your painting, as it has been for artists of all kinds since painting began. When you have studied your model and, with pencil, pen or brush, captured all its secrets on paper, change its position and start again. You cannot do enough, and after thirty years of painting wildlife, I still cannot do enough drawing from life.

Fig. 13 Doe rat: the approach, in watercolour, to a studio
specimen set up on blocks

FORM, PROPORTION AND PATTERN

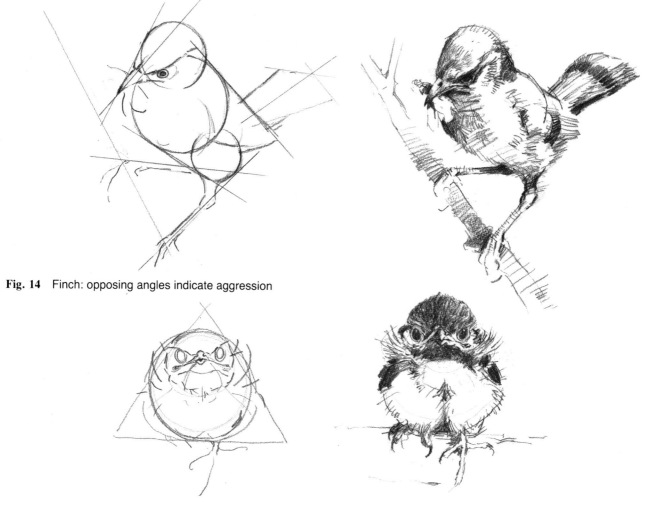

Fig. 14 Finch: opposing angles indicate aggression

Fig. 15 Fledgling: inter-relating lines indicate a passive attitude

When you begin sketching wildlife you will observe that the form of your animal subjects can be quickly pencilled in as a series of simple geometric shapes, rectangles, triangles and circles. The way in which form and proportion help express an animal's mood can also be suggested initially using this visual shorthand. Lines of tension are not usually drawn in, but with the drawing of the finch (**fig. 14**) I have shown the major lines to demonstrate that strongly opposing angles provide an aggressive expression, whereas compact and inter-relating lines, as with the fledgling (**fig. 15**), give a soft appearance. The relationships between the masses, illustrated in the drawing of the bank vole (**fig. 17**), enhance the creature's essential character.

The profile or outline of an animal will suggest that animal's attitude. An angular, taut silhouette will ' speak of tension and anger. Hunched shoulders and open mouths suggest threat or warning; a head turned sharply at right-angles to the body suggests fear. A soft, rounded, solid profile suggests content and calm.

Within the profile (the outline), there are surface patterns and surface textures. These behave in very specific ways as they follow the curves and contours of an animal's body, and some study will show you how. A strongly marked creature, like the serval (**fig. 16**), provides us, most obviously, with an example of how patterns alter and flatten as they follow a curved surface. A circle begins to distort as it turns away from the viewer, forming narrower and narrower elipses until, at the periphery of the curve (that point which approximates to the horizon on land), it appears as a straight line. Flat colour can be seen as a most subtle arrangement of mounds and curves simply by manipulating the superficial patterns.

The bank vole (**fig. 17**) is a triangle of simple forms when its bulk is analysed. It has no continuous patterning with which to suggest contour but its surface texture can be used in a similar way. The pattern made by fur as it curves away from the light source and ends in shadow can be readily used to indicate three dimensions.

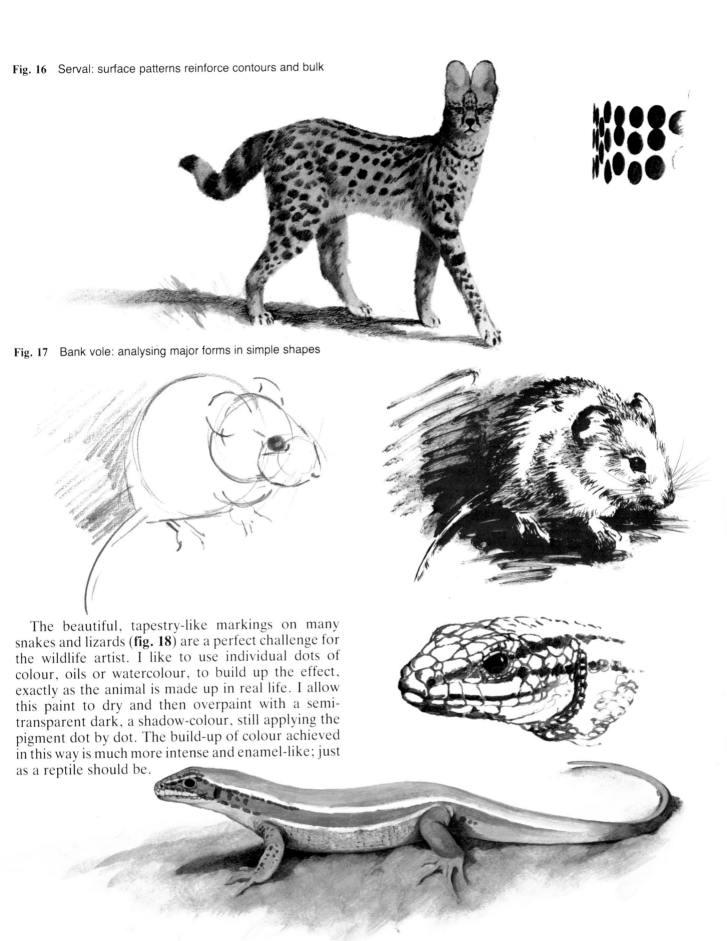

Fig. 16 Serval: surface patterns reinforce contours and bulk

Fig. 17 Bank vole: analysing major forms in simple shapes

The beautiful, tapestry-like markings on many snakes and lizards (**fig. 18**) are a perfect challenge for the wildlife artist. I like to use individual dots of colour, oils or watercolour, to build up the effect, exactly as the animal is made up in real life. I allow this paint to dry and then overpaint with a semi-transparent dark, a shadow-colour, still applying the pigment dot by dot. The build-up of colour achieved in this way is much more intense and enamel-like; just as a reptile should be.

Fig. 18 Lizard: the use of surface patterns to enhance form and proportion

23

MOVEMENT

All animals have a gait which is peculiar to them alone: the stoat's snake-like scurry punctuated with sudden periscopic pauses; the loping, almost lazy bound of the hare; the quick trot of the fox. You must represent these accurately for each breed if your finished work is to be of any authority.

Looking at the drawings of the deer opposite (**figs. 19–21**), you can see the quite different forms that extended or contracted muscles make in the process of action. Once you have established the attitude of your subject, you must make sure that the musculature is modelled in the correct way for the pose. As a general rule, bent limbs carry bunched or knotted muscles which will be clearly defined by highlight and shadow; an overall rounded feeling should be aimed for. Straight or stretched limbs look sleek and flat, and muscle shapes should be smooth and fluid, running together without much shadow contrast. The stag descending (**fig. 19**) has all the body weight on the front legs and is using muscle control to maintain an awkward position. In **fig. 20** the reverse of the above is true. Because of the extreme nature of the animal's situation, the muscles are bunched and clearly defined although the limbs are straight. This helps to strengthen the mood of the work and suggests tension in the composition. As with all detail, accuracy is essential if it is to lend any authority to the portrayal. Throughout the history of animal art, the paintings which have sought out the essential rather than the superficial have been of most lasting success.

Fig. 19

Fig. 20

Studies of changing muscle forms during movement

Fig. 21 Running deer: the major forms blocked in with wash

ANATOMY OF FISH

The underlying skeleton of a fish describes its proportions, its form and its action in a precise and inviolate way. The soft, flexible areas such as the belly and throat are supported by the ribs and skull without having any rigidity from bones passing through them. They are, therefore, of variable shape and size and, if twisted or folded, will show creases on the skin surface. The back (dorsal) and tail (caudal) muscles are heavily boned with fine interlocking spines originating at the vertebrae and curving out and back through these tissues. The skull is a solid shell of bone, very near the surface and allowing no flexibility whatsoever.

Once the anatomy here (**fig. 22**) is clearly understood, and the exterior detailing of a given species (in this case a common carp) is noted accurately, you should be able to draw your fish from any angle and in any shape you wish. Reduce your subject to a few essential lines and you have your proportions (**fig. 23**). Add shading and tone and you achieve form (**fig. 24**). So, if you want to show your fish leaping and twisting, know your skeleton. I think one of the nicest ways to study a fish's bone structure is as you carefully separate it from the flesh on a dinner plate; but if you can get hold of a fish, or if you can get to a museum where you can take a sketchbook, a 5 mm HB automatic pencil and a kneadable rubber and see one on display, then a careful drawing will do more for your knowledge of animal structure than twenty written works. Be very strict with yourself, however, and get your drawing *absolutely* correct, counting the bones and getting the number right, the proportions accurate, and the angles, most importantly, showing the natural line that the overlay of muscles will take when you come to paint or draw a less studied subject.

Like a beautiful engine or a great building, the exterior is arrived at only after a real awareness of the underlying structure and a knowledge of the insides are achieved. While these 'foundations' are unseen, and often unappreciated, yet their absence or an inadequate understanding of their function leaves the finished work lacking in authority and, somehow, unsatisfactory to the viewer.

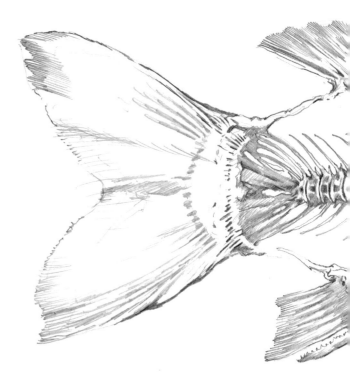

Fig. 22 Common carp: the underlying frame

Fig. 23 Basic proportions

Fig. 24 The textures, tones and forms which clothe the skeleton

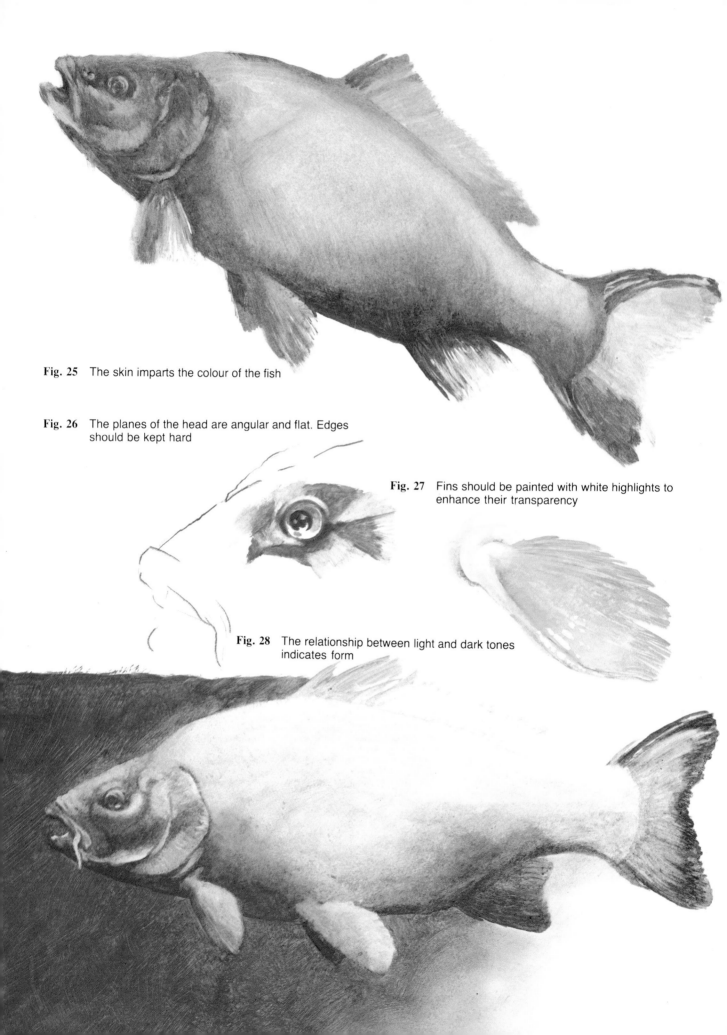

Fig. 25 The skin imparts the colour of the fish

Fig. 26 The planes of the head are angular and flat. Edges should be kept hard

Fig. 27 Fins should be painted with white highlights to enhance their transparency

Fig. 28 The relationship between light and dark tones indicates form

STUDYING YOUR SUBJECT

When approaching the subject of your picture and contemplating the technique most suitable and the process of painting, it is often of help to consider the actual structure of your creature. Under the scales of a fish there is a leathery, smooth skin, and it is this which imparts the colour (**fig. 25**) – the scales are transparent in the main, and have a speckled, reflective edge. The contours of the fish, and their reaction to the light source, describe the animal's form (**fig. 28**). There we are: three parts of the fish, easily reproduced, one on top of the other, in paint.

Using oils or watercolour, begin with the forms in a dark colour on white. Overlay the general colour of the fish, keeping the lighter parts of the form crisp and clean, and merging your colour into the background darks where you cover shading. Overpaint the scales, one at a time, in long, lateral rows, reflecting the general colour, and painting white (you can lay this on in a solid mass) for the underparts. This gives you surface texture and pattern, and the undulations of the rows reinforce the form, the 'roundness' of your fish. Paint any pattern the fish carries as you would build up a mosaic: use small dots of colour as 'tessare' (the individual pieces of coloured material which make up a mosaic). Your fish should now be finished, save for highlights. Any wet, slippery object will throw off pure white highlights – study the fishmonger's slab! The whole can appear a little crude, however, and it is necessary to smooth layers of overpainting into each other with a fan brush, say a Dalon Series D.55 No. 3, to achieve subtlety and realism.

Fig. 29   The technique of painting scales

Fig. 30   Fish float! A strong shadow lifts your subject away from its surroundings

ANATOMY OF BIRDS IN FLIGHT

The curvature of a bird's wings depends on the flying (down) stroke, or the retrieving (up) stroke. A bird gains lift and forward flying speed by pushing down hard with both wings and dipping down, slightly, by using the tail. If you paint a bird coming in to land, it would look wrong seen on a down stroke, the stroke of acceleration. Similarly, if you paint a bird taking off, it would look wrong seen on an up stroke, the stroke of deceleration or braking. Think carefully of the circumstances you place your subject in and get the details right.

The striking owl (**fig. 31**) is seen in an extreme position, at the peak of physical effort and concentration. A look at the skeleton (**fig. 32**) will show you that these remarkable contortions in no way disobey the laws and conditions of the creature's anatomy, indicating just how articulated a wild animal's structure can be. Within an accurate framework underlying the finished form, there is ample opportunity to find images or compositions of remarkable impact.

Fig. 31

Fig. 32 Owl: a thorough study of the skeleton will give you confidence when handling extreme action

FIELD NOTES

Fig. 33 Sparrowhawk: identification sketch

Fig. 34 First rough sketch of the scene

Much preparatory work can be done at home before you venture out into the field with pencil and sketchbook. I know of a sparrowhawk's nest locally, and decided to make use of the site for a picture. Before I went out, I drew an outline of the bird (copied roughly from a bird identification book such as *Collins Field Guide to British Birds*) in strong, simple lines (**fig. 33**). I would fill this in with more precise detail in the field. Then I sketched a rough outline of the composition I wanted and headed separate sheets of my sketchbook with the necessary components: nest, foliage, sky, branches – every detail that might enhance my composition had a page to itself.

Once in the field, and hidden beneath the sparrowhawk's nest, I positioned my equipment around me so as to keep movement to a minimum. The first drawing was a general view of the nest and surroundings and, very lucky this time, the male sparrowhawk (musket) alighting several times to feed his brooding mate (**fig. 34**). I flipped back the pages of my sketchbook to write in some plumage details on my ready-drawn dummy. As one observes a site like this for a period of time, one begins to identify the eccentric or the unusual in one's field of view. Here, the hawks had included the red and white cardboard of a cigarette packet in the structure of the nest, and it struck an incongruous note – a device which might well work in a picture to highlight the subject. All these details should be drawn and described.

Always remember to keep a weather eye on good background material for your paintings: bark, rock, earth banks with roots, plants, branches, posts, gates,

water margins, nests – the list is endless. Keep notes on colour and collect samples of leaves, twigs, and the like, from your background scene, to give you a base colour guide. Also record the creatures you might expect to see in any environment you consider worth noting, and look around for actual signs of the wildlife which has frequented your site. The more knowledge you acquire, the better your work will be. When you feel happy with the amount of field work done, return to your studio and start cross-referencing with photographs of your subject from books and natural-history magazines, and build up a set of detail drawings which describe any aspect of your picture which demands absolute accuracy (**fig. 35**).

By now you should have a very clear picture in your mind of what your finished piece will look like. Make a drawing, to size, of your composition and include, in as much detail as possible, all the elements you have gathered from your field trips and your research (**fig. 36**). It is now that you will uncover any weakness in your composition and can begin 'honing' or 'fining' your picture: rounding out the work with supporting detail; altering the attitude of your subject a little here, a little there; sharpening the look of the thing so as to get the maximum effect from your images.

A sequence from field to finished drawing in the studio allows you time and practice to get to the heart of your subject. As you work on you will familiarize yourself with all aspects of your picture, and by the time you come to put paint on paper or canvas you should know, in every particular, the drawing, the composition, the sequence of painting and the degree of finish that you require to achieve your goal.

Fig. 35 Detail drawings

Fig. 36 Finished studio rough

STUDY OF FEATHERS

This classic study (in oils) for your reference library, detailing a bird's wing, will give you much more information than simply shape and colour. The relationships between colours can be projected on to the canvas as a guide to colour over the whole of your painting, and the proportions of bright detail to drab background can be ascertained and used as a guide for your work in general. The careful study of these details of nature in this way can give you valuable guidelines which you will be able to apply to all aspects of your art.

Pin up your model close to the work surface and sit down comfortably to study it. Look and concentrate for a while, getting a general feel of the overall colours, and then decide how you can achieve an accurate result with the *least* number of tube colours possible, squeezing a small amount of each (about the size of a pea) on to the sides of your palette (**fig. 37**). Use a pencil brush (Dalon D.77 No. 3 or 4 is about right) and mix a light background colour to base your work. (If you feel unhappy about drawing straight on to the paper with a brush, draw a faint outline with an HB fine point first.) Keep your paint thin and transparent and mix only with diluent (turps substitute or white spirit) – *no oil*! Let the brush make its own feather effect by pushing the paint around with flicks and short strokes, and let the brush hairs spread and separate. The colour should be no more than tinted spirit, very transparent (**fig. 37**). Work back from the wing tips with a dark colour (**fig. 38 and 39**), then overlay with a solid white to give the barred effect (**fig. 40**); let the colours blend at the edges on the paper. Fill in the dark patterns on the small underwing feathers and then paint up to them with white. Allow an hour for drying, then, using a very transparent brown with a *hint* of blue, brush in the shading with a small fan (**fig. 40**). If you notice colour coming off and mixing with your shadow colour, stop and leave to dry more. Finish with a small pencil brush (Dalon D.77 No. 1) by outlining and sharpening up details and edges where necessary. Wait two days, then fix with a matt spray.

Fig. 37

Fig. 38 First stage

Fig. 39 Second stage

Fig. 40 Finished stage

PAINTING BUTTERFLIES

Fig. 41 Field sketches

There are certain subjects which require a special approach and are very demanding of an artist's technique. Moths and butterflies are the most subtle and delicately marked of all insects, and their caterpillars are similarly patterned and shaded. Careful observation and plenty of drawings in your field notebook must come before you can approach butterfly painting (**fig. 41**). Study the way the wings appear from different angles and try to avoid the obvious symmetrical pose with both wings laid flat. Detail is essential with insects: make as many different drawings of detail as you can and make them quite large, say four times larger than life. The intricate structures should be carefully drawn with an HB pencil on white cartridge.

Their size presents a problem to begin with and, generally, I like to compose a picture including moths or butterflies by having a wide, drab backdrop with the insects as exquisite droplets of brilliant colour placed carefully within the picture plane but quite small and precise. The background needs research as most butterflies are specific to certain plants. It is a good idea to make notes on foliage and any other features in your subject's immediate surroundings.

Once you know your butterfly and the relevant foliage, paint in with a solid, dark tone, a background colour which complements your subject. The brightly coloured Vanessids (Red Admiral, Emperor, etc.) can take a strong range of good greens (**fig. 45**), but the Fritillaries or Meadow Browns would be overpowered by these and need a much more neutral tone; green-brown or amber-brown would enhance and heighten the impact of these tiny brown/red butterflies, and an underlying shadow will throw the subject into relief.

The patterns on the wings are made up of minute scales, each a distinct colour, and, if you can, you should reproduce these patterns similarly with paint (**fig. 42**). Painting two butterflies together gives you the opportunity to show the underwing as well as the dorsal colour, but always work from actual specimens when attempting this particular scene.

Caterpillars (**fig. 43**) must be accurately drawn and coloured, too, and should be identifiable as to type. Use an HB pencil to get detail and watercolour to make a side-view reference picture for your library. Look up the animal's proper name and label your painting with it.

Fig. 43

Fig. 42 Swallowtail: detailed study of the wing colour and pattern

Fig. 44 Try to avoid the obvious symmetrical pose

Fig. 45

37

COMPOSITION AND INTERPRETATION

Fig. 46 Rabbits and stoats: acquiring a reference library with pencil sketches in the field

I can give no better advice as you consider what to paint than to choose a subject you know. Painting a wildlife picture is, in part, a question of using your artistic skills to reveal something of nature which the viewer would otherwise not be privy to, and it is the responsibility of the artist not to misrepresent his subjects but to enhance and add to the viewer's awareness of them. It is difficult enough coping with the practical problems of technique without adding to the task. A subject you are familiar with will also give you confidence in drawing, painting and scale.

Suppose the scenario for your canvas is a stoat and a rabbit: an elusive scene that few can have witnessed at first hand. Which animal do you feature most prominently? The rabbit, unsuspecting, browsing in the foreground, or the sinister stoat, an ominous shadow in the rear? Or do you paint the stoat almost filling the frame? Do you intertwine the two forms almost as a heraldic device, implying the more profound relationship of the two creatures in the wild? These are the kind of questions every artist must ask himself when planning a composition of this kind.

In this instance, I felt that the character of each animal should be delineated. The stoat I wished to appear lithe and ruthless, the arch predator, crouched and determined (perhaps with a glitter of white as the fangs appear behind the smile). The rabbit was more difficult; no longer warm and fecund, chewing dandelion or sorrel, enjoying the summer heat, but the quarry, hunted and caught, with an awareness of its part having been played and resignation in its eye. There was a vacancy of expression in the rabbit which I wanted to paint to complement and contrast with the glittering ferocity which the lip-licking stoat imparted (**fig. 47**).

Begin with sketchbook and pencil and start playing with shapes taken from your field notes, establishing scale between the principals (rabbits are bigger than stoats, but by how much?) and rhythm (**fig. 46**). If you cannot find a stoat in the field you may have to resort to photographs. Think of the light and dark of the backdrop as you position your subjects within the picture plane; think also of the most advantageous point of view – choose one that most helps the impact of your scene. Can your viewpoint be enhanced by a close-up? Do you want to contrast the lovely landscape with the teeth and claws? Think of yourself as an architect drawing up a groundplan before attempting to build the reality. I like to consider the subject of a picture as I might chance across it in the wild: a fleeting glimpse of an animal poised before flight. Such an image should be fixed as soon as possible in the sketch form with notes. Your painting should attempt to subdue the less important parts of the picture whilst spotlighting the most relevant details. I sometimes use a bright shaft of light in an otherwise shaded scene to leave absolutely no doubt as to the painting's focal point. This use of shadow and illumination is a very useful tool in the wildlife artist's range of techniques, considering the elusive nature of his subjects. Bearing in mind the overall tone of the piece, begin sketching in these darks and lights in your composition (**fig. 48**).

The background components can be reduced to textures and forms of an almost abstract nature at this point. Positive lines, such as branches or reeds, and negatives such as shadows or spaces, join together to form pointers or indicate direction. They are valuable devices for leading the view to the chosen centre of the composition, in this case the glitter in the stoat's eye. Establish bold lines. Do not be half-hearted about relationships. Do not allow forms to touch just at the edges as this is awkward, but keep them well apart or make them overlap strongly. Make two cut-out shapes representing the stoat and the rabbit and move them about until you discover the most readable and exciting position with curves and lines flowing. Move a leg here or a head there, if it helps; do not be limited to your original pose if it conflicts with its counterpart, however pleased you are with that shape in isolation. Rhythms should be achieved in tones of light and shade. The attitude of a creature when frozen in two dimensions must suggest the pace and vitality of the living animal; the stoat is lithe and fluid, the rabbit stolid and shy. There is always a place for deliberately rendering a subject out of character for the sake of tension, but be careful – like garlic in a good meal, use sparingly.

Fig. 47

Fig. 48 Pencil sketch of the composition

You are now ready to start painting. Clear a space for your reference material – photographs, specimens or whatever – and make sure your equipment is prepared. Having established the composition after experimenting with pencil and sketchbook, and deciding to work in oils, the major lines and shapes must be transferred to the canvas. I use one of two methods: I cover the back of my rough drawing with pencil shading (a Black Beauty is useful here), position the sketch on the canvas, and go over all the main lines and forms with an HB pencil. This draws through on to the painting surface rather like a carbon

Fig. 49 Establishing the light and dark tones

copy. The other method, for work that needs to be scaled up in size, is to draw a grid of squares over the rough sketch, then an equal number of squares of sufficient size to cover the canvas. Each small square on the sketch can be accurately redrawn in its corresponding large square on the painting surface. Once the rough is transferred, I like to fill out the layout with charcoal, concentrating on the main areas of light and shade. This would be wrong for watercolour as the charcoal would dirty the subtle washes, but oil assimilates charcoal quite readily.

The overall colour of **fig. 49** is a green-brown, so I mixed a dark tone with Vandyke Brown and Prussian Blue and started painting in the shaded areas with a Dalon D.22 $\frac{1}{2}$ inch flat. When this was complete, I stood back to see, for the first time, the composition as a whole. It was at this point that I started changing a line here or a shape there, beginning to fine the work as I went along. Never be strict about following original lines; it is not until the brush begins to bring out the images on the canvas that weaknesses can be remedied or additions made for improvement. Be flexible and prepared to change and adapt as your work progresses.

I worked into the picture while the shadow colour was still retrievable to blend colour and texture into shadow. (Although apparently dry, the paint was still soft enough to be made fluid again when brushed with turpentine. The more linseed oil in the original colour mix, the longer it will stay 'retrievable'.) The painting was now at the stage shown outside the central square, with detail beginning to emerge and colour being enhanced (**fig. 50**). In some parts of the background this soft focus and vague detail was as far as I would go, preferring to save the high finish and strong detail for the important central area of the picture.

The stoat and the rabbit's head, and the way that these two intertwine, make a clear statement about the creatures and their relationship in the wild. The pose is the traditional one for victor and vanquished and this area of the painting contains the essence of the work, so I concentrated the strongest painting here. I brushed in the shaded fur with a Dalon D.66 No. 1, teasing out the earlier shadow colour and blending the two. Into the wet paint of the shadow fur I painted the lighter shades until I was painting almost white fur in strong illumination. These areas were blended into one another so as to give an even transposition from dark to light.

The face of the stoat is the very centre of the piece and was painted with most strength. I painted in the overall rust colour first, then into this colour placed the eye and the inside of the mouth with Lamp Black, straight from the tube. The white fur was painted on so as to use the dark underpainting as shading and modelling for the features; by painting white on with a single stroke it remained clean white, but by using more than one stroke and pushing the paint about, the undercolour started coming to the surface and 'shaded' the white. The resulting tones give a remarkably accurate rendering of fur and perfectly describe the creature's facial expression. The fine hairs on the muzzle and brows were made by scratching with a compass point; a finer and sharper effect than a paintbrush could achieve. The highlights in the eye are Titanium White straight from the tube, dotted in with the point of a Dalon D.77 No. 000.

At this stage I looked at the work as a finished piece; as a whole. I reinforced the shading around the subjects so as to bring them well forward, and worked on odd details of grass, background and subject until I was satisfied that I needed to go no further. The work was put away flat and left to dry thoroughly. After a week or two, I signed the picture and varnished it.

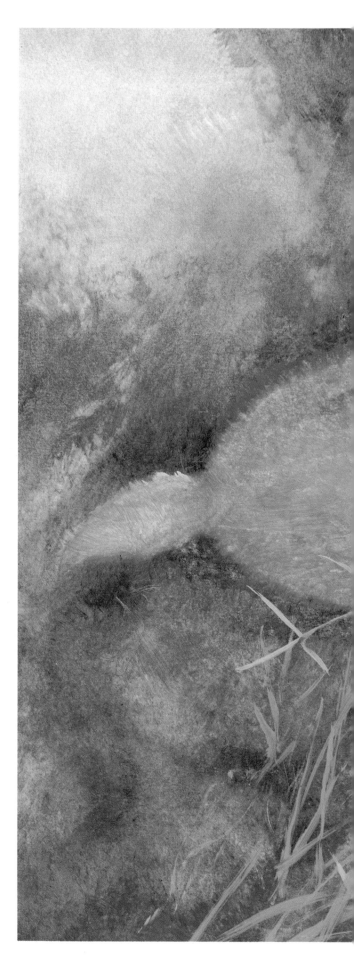

Fig. 50 Developing colour, texture and detail

DRAWING IN THE FIELD

Certain circumstances will not allow you merely to sketch in pencil or charcoal and then return to your studio to work up your painting to a finish. Sometimes you will need more studied observation on site. The trout stream is a classic example. Fish appear fleetingly, if at all, and can only really be drawn from memory. When dealing with a subject like this, stand and watch for as long as you can – patience here can be worth more than its own reward. Build up a mental picture of your fish, as you watch them, and look for regular or recurring patterns of action. A rising trout comes straight to the surface then curves into a U shape to dart back to the bottom. Fish holding their position in a current, wriggle constantly in a shallow S shape, while fish holding their position in still water, stay very straight, using only the movement of their fins. While these images and observations are fresh in your mind, try putting them down on paper (**fig. 51**). Pencil in essential lines quickly and in one stroke (the line from the fish's nose, down the centre of the back to the tail, is the only one you need worry about here), attempting the fluid movement of the creature itself. Draw in possible positions of fins. If your sketches are unsatisfactory to start with, stop drawing and start looking again. Eventually you will have a few pages of fish in all manner of poses. Even if you do not have the fish there that you need for your painting, by now you will know so well how these creatures move that you will be able to draw it from memory.

The water, water-weeds and banks are permanent fixtures, yet a pencil sketch can rarely carry enough information about such a scene, so an oil sketch, done on the spot, is needed. For this, use a flat, smooth-surfaced card (Bristol board is good) cut to a convenient size to carry (A4). Card absorbs oil and spirit quite quickly and your sketch will dry nicely before packing to carry home. The use of a brush handle or a bamboo scraping tool is much more effective on a smooth surface and much of your sketching will be of this type; brushing on solid areas of colour and then scraping back to the natural white surface beneath. Be quick and bold as you work. It is the impression you wish to capture, not the detail. Look and look again as you work.

Make sure you establish the main areas of light and dark, and begin to distinguish between below and above the water surface. Try to capture the distortions that an irregular water surface imparts to solid

Fig. 51   Trout: the field sketch in charcoal pencil

Fig. 52 First stage

Fig. 53 Second stage

Fig. 54 Finished stage

objects seen beneath it. To do this successfully, make your brush behave like the water itself. Apply a dark colour, representing the overall tone and hue of the water, and with a scribe or scoring tool scrape the forms of the weeds into the wet paint (the dark colour may need lubricating with a little linseed oil, once or twice, to keep it from drying out), building up a general impression of the masses and forms made by the water-flow on the weedbed (**fig. 52**). Using a dry fan brush, Dalon D.55 No. 2, draw a series of zig-zag strokes across the line of the weeds, which will reproduce the effect of ripples by distorting the lines of the weeds. With a small pencil brush, Dalon D.77 No. 1, loaded with a pale green, wriggle in the colour of the weeds, following the distorted lines of the fan-brushed base colour. Follow this procedure over the whole of the picture area, continually stopping to blur edges and distress and distort hard lines with your No. 2 fan (**fig. 53**). In my sketch I made the rising trout the focal point and I wanted the radiating rings of water from this rise to enhance the fish like a halo. I scraped the series of elipses (circles seen in perspective) with my brush handle and softened them with the No. 2 fan.

Now for the fish themselves (**fig. 54**). There is a problem with painting fish. The light shines on them from above, where they are dark coloured, and they are in shadow on the underside, where they are light coloured. So, we must paint the white in shadow and the dark illuminated. Observation of fish in water is the only answer to this problem, and you will soon see that, in certain lights and at certain angles, the fish can be lighter above than below. In my sketch, however, with a point of view from fairly high above, the relationship of light and shade to colour is dark above and lighter below, as one would expect. Paint in your light colour, then the dark, merge the two colours with a Dalon D.88 $\frac{1}{4}$ inch, then dot in the pattern on the flanks of the fish. Blur and soften by flicking your No. 2 fan over the whole surface, and repoint (make sharp and clear again) any areas that you feel need precision and clarity, such as the heads of the fish. Dot in highlights with Titanium White lifted straight from the tube and soften these by fanning the wet paint diagonally left top to right bottom, then left bottom to right top. Keep a light touch and a free-moving hand working from the wrist.

This sketch took me less than ten minutes at the riverbank and all the materials were carried in a small box easily contained in a satchel. The paper was Bristol board mounted on offcuts of corrugated card (cut from the clean, flat sides of cardboard boxes) with an aerosol adhesive. The end result, in conjunction with photographs of weed and water detail, and text-book references for the fish, contained everything that I needed before starting on a finished work back in the studio.

THE DEGREE OF FINISH

Many people see wildlife painting only as very highly finished and photographically realistic. However, sketchy impressions can often convey much more precisely the nature or form of your subject and, after all, wild creatures are usually seen only as a series of fleeting images conveying an 'impression' of form rather than a clear description. Any artist will tell you that one of the most useful skills you can develop is the ability to recognize when your piece of work is finished – knowing when to stop. When I say finished, I must underline that I do not necessarily use the word in the sense of everything being complete; a few quick lines describing a running fox can be 'finished' as a picture. When a painting says everything you wish it to say about your subject, any further painting is merely embroidery and will only distract the viewer.

The picture of an otter was started with a conté pencil drawing (**fig. 55**) taken to a fairly high degree of detail. Colour washes in oils or watercolour were then applied, beginning the process of building up colour in layers. Darker colours, as for the deep water behind the lily pads, were strengthened with heavier washes until the desired degree of opacity (the 'solidness' of a colour) was achieved (**fig. 56**). The form of the animal was flashed in with ragged strokes, using a dark shading colour and a medium round-ended brush, and these were blended into the background with a fan brush to give the indistinct, underwater feel. The lily pads were given detail – ribs and shading – with a No. 2 or 3 round-ended brush. Highlights were sketched in (**fig. 57**), and as I was dealing with moving water, the brush (in this case a fairly large pencil brush) had to be kept loose and fluid. The difference between fur under water and above it had to be made clear (this defines the plane of the water surface as well) and colour was the simplest method of achieving this. The final section (**fig. 58**) shows high finish. The diffused highlights in the foreground were painted by 'pointing' – thick dots of pure white were put on the canvas and then 'flared' with a small fan brush whisked gently back and forth across the points of white along both diagonals. The fur about the otter's face was painted with a fine pencil brush (No. 0), applying the colour in strokes along the lie of the pelt and shading to bring out the forms of the face. The eyes were clearly delineated and the highlights put in, using pure white. The painting was complete.

However, whether the last stage (**fig. 58**) – or come to that, **fig. 56.** or **fig. 57** – although highly finished, says any more about otters than the original conté drawing (**fig. 55**) is debatable. I suspect not.

Fig. 55 First stage

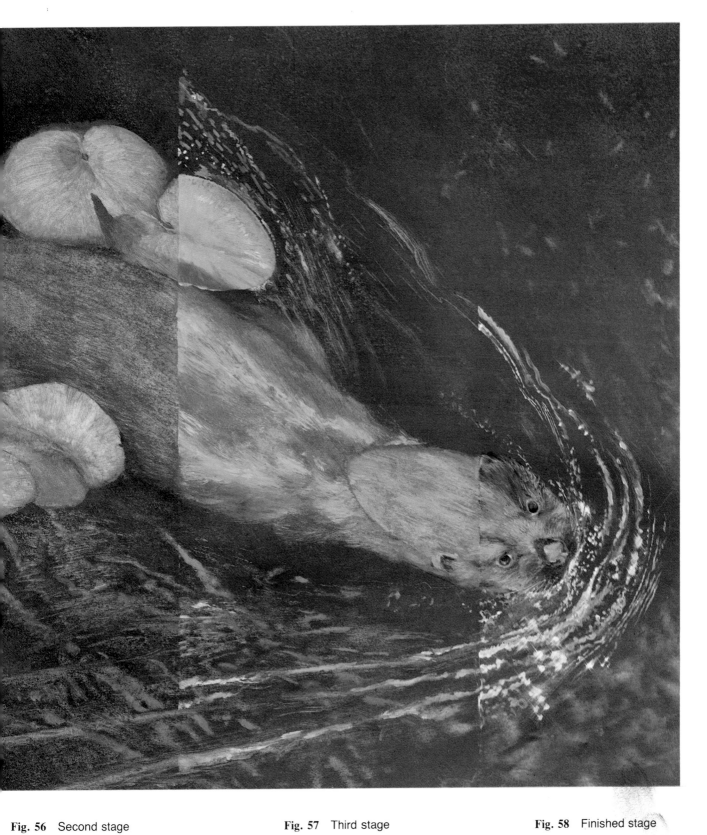

Fig. 56 Second stage   **Fig. 57** Third stage   **Fig. 58** Finished stage

SHORELINE SNIPE

Fig. 59 Establishing the scale of the subject in relation to the background

Now you have had some practice at drawing specimens at your table, you will be able to collect field notes in preparation for a finished work. Let us go step by step through the process of translating a scene into an oil painting.

The scene will probably have suggested itself as the basis of a picture if you are familiar with it (stick to what you know!) either because of a sudden change of light or, as in the case of the seashore scene here, the arrival into a known landscape of some unusual visitors. The flock of snipe stayed for several days and I studied them with binoculars for a day before going out with a pad and a 5 mm HB propelling pencil (always with a sharp point) to get some sketches.

Shapes and patterns as the birds fly in groups; details and notes – length of wing, bill, body, etc.; size and position relative to the horizon and tideline; atmosphere and lighting; notes on colour: all this information was needed (**figs. 59 and 60**). As you study to collect such information you are absorbing the overall feeling of the place. Written notes are just as useful as drawings, and if you have a watercolour box, paint a spectrum that sums up the colour of the scene. In my painting (**fig. 61**), amber, grey-green and brown, with peripheral splashes of blue and reflected white light, were all I needed. Do not try to use every colour in your box in every picture you paint. Less can very often be more.

Fig. 60 Preliminary field sketches

Fig. 61 Establishing the colour scheme

Back in the studio, after toying with a sketchbook of white cartridge and a 6B pencil and trying out different views, I had a fairly clear idea that my picture would be a clear, brightly lit, but slightly wintry seascape, with my snipe, like a litter of windblown autumn leaves, cascading across it as they coast down to land. I wanted to capture the overall pattern of their flight, rather than detail, so I could light them strongly – some almost silhouettes – as if by a high sun. This was also very dramatic and provided a strong, dark pattern against a soft, pale ground. The birds cut very positively across the strong horizontals made by the sea. A soft reflective feel to the sand made the whole background very watery, also in contrast to the snipe.

I quickly sketched in the birds, and when the flock was right – the right number and weight – I tried on a piece of tracing paper various possibilities for the horizon and tideline. When satisfied, I marked them in on the watercolour and began painting (**fig. 62**). I painted in the sea, the sand and the sky with thin washes, building up to the intensity I wanted, using a generous sable ($\frac{1}{2}$ inch). As the pencil lines would show through I could paint right across the picture – I did not try to paint round the birds. Then, with a No. 1 pencil brush I sketched in the shadows in brown, and when correct in strength, I used just a wet brush to tease the brown out over the remaining areas of the birds. I was now familiar with my composition to the point where my finished oil painting could be executed with an absolutely clear idea as to the order of work, the colours involved and any alterations or corrections that might be required. I had also eliminated the awful business of staring at a completely blank canvas with a brain to match. An image needs time to settle, especially for the person responsible for creating it, so I gave myself some time to study the picture before I started on my canvas. I put it out of sight for a while then came back to it fresh. I sometimes look at my work reflected in a mirror – you will be surprised how fresh your view of a piece of work can be by using this trick.

Fig. 62 Watercolour studio sketch

I like to transfer a very precise composition like *Shoreline Snipe* in a very precise way. Tracing the major lines and marks off the watercolour, I began to redraw them on to canvas primed with gesso (a creamy plaster giving a smooth, paperlike surface), using a 2H pencil and carbon paper. The sky was painted in one 'pass', using the watercolour pinned to the board to the left of the canvas for reference. I mixed colour as near to the watercolour as possible then put it on the canvas with a Dalon $\frac{1}{2}$ inch flat. Texture and inconsistent paint density came automatically as the brush worked across the gesso. I blended out those textures which I did not want with a Dalon No. 6 fan but some enhanced my painting beautifully and these I kept in – always look out for the 'happy accident'! I used a maul-stick 1 metre (1 yd) long to help me rule in the horizon across the canvas with a Dalon No. 3 flat, and then painted the sea from this point down. Remember that distance softens colour; I painted with increasing intensity as I came towards the tideline. I left the waves until the sand was painted in. By using colours from the sky, I could achieve a reflective surface on the sand (always softening and blending with a fan) and the desired wetness. The waves were painted with pure white, one side being left hard, the other blended out. A touch of shadow between the leading edge of the waves and the wet sand seated the water firmly on top of the land, where it belonged.

By this time, only the birds remained. An exact copy of my practice with the watercolour sketch, building up to just the right strength and opacity, achieved the correct result, and by being careful to paint all overlapping forms in the correct order, I completed the painting (**fig. 63**). If any areas of a finished picture seem harsh or raw, wait until the paint is just going off and then dust all over with a large fan, making doubly sure that it is dust-free and clean. Then, only a signature is lacking.

Fig. 63   *Shoreline Snipe*: finished oil

SHORELINE SNIPE

GALLERY:
OBSERVATIONS AND DETAILS

Fig. 64 *Heron*

The pictures here are all works which were commissioned or painted to a commercial brief, for publishers or industry. They have a superficial similarity, being the work of one artist, yet each one makes a special point and represents the solution to a different problem.

I have described each picture bearing in mind its one special facet, whether that be the technique of painting, unusual composition, or unexpected point of view. A painting can, and perhaps should, contain all of these points, yet these pictures have been selected because each one is an example of how one particular problem was solved. They were all achieved using the methods and techniques described in the preceding chapters, and where details are illustrated they are shown at actual size.

The heron (**fig. 64**) is a creature hardly ever seen at close quarters. This leaves the artist with two possibilities: to represent the bird in a natural way and paint it as it would naturally be seen; or to give the viewer the benefit of the artist's ability to get behind the scenes or into otherwise closed places. I felt that this bird was distinctive enough not to get lost in the wider view, and I consequently saw it as part of a much larger landscape. The three main elements – bird, tree and background – are each quite distinct in texture and act as foils, one against the others. Another important consideration to be taken into account is the size of the bird: big enough to carry some degree of detail (especially about the head), yet small enough within the picture plan to seem hidden and secret.

The bee-eater (**fig. 65**) is not only exotic in colour and form, but in life-style. No background was necessary in this painting except for a suitable overall drab to offset the jewel-like quality of the bird, so I painted an earth bank, grey in general colour and featureless save for a strong diagonal to 'raise' the bird off the canvas. The hole in the bank, obvious home of the bees, gives a reason for the action taking place. The bird was painted in flat colours as this is how the creature would be seen flitting by. One wing was left unpainted: the 'happy accident' which lent some life to an otherwise stiff watercolour composition.

The detail of the bee (**fig. 66**) shows another example of the 'happy accident'. I tried painting the flashing wings of the flying insect several times and found it most difficult to resolve properly. I decided to erase what I had painted with a little water and begin again. I removed the water with my finger and discovered that the smudgy fingerprint, with a flash of white paper showing through, was just the effect I wanted.

Fig. 66

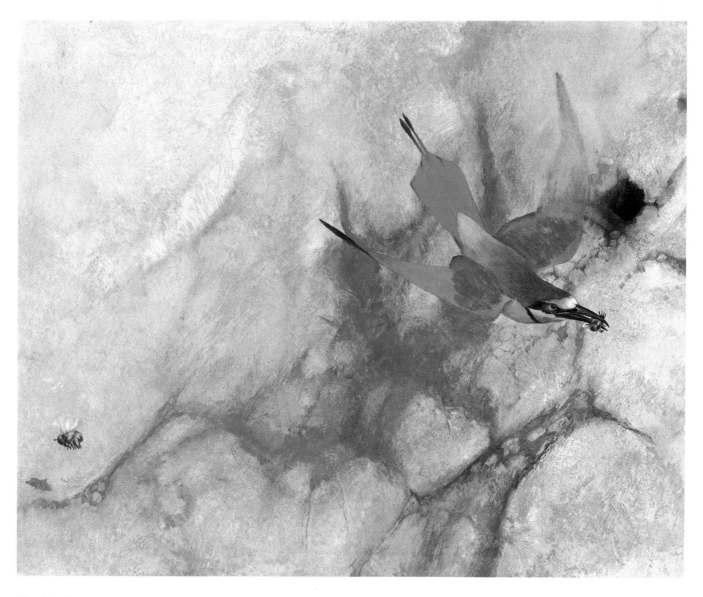

Fig. 65   *Bee-eater*

This painting (**fig. 67**), from Conoco's 1985 calendar, presented me with a particularly unusual problem. As a subject for a wildlife painting, the toad, I must admit, would not spring immediately to mind. Being one of the twelve required 'hunter and hunted' subjects, however, it was necessary to look closely at the animal and to discover some aspect of it which was aesthetically acceptable. This proved harder than I expected and I was beginning to despair of the piece when one of those 'happy accidents' occurred and the picture was set: I was gardening, and a toad walked slowly into the sunlight from under a clump of dock and posed most professionally at my feet; the play of light on the warty skin and the flecks of orange fire in its eyes turned the creature into a thing of jade and amber, quite perfect! I had already assembled details of toads from photographs and earlier drawings, so I had only to carry this image in my mind's eye and bring it to the studio.

I started this oil painting by laying Vandyke Brown on the paper with a Dalon 1 inch flat and working shapes into it with a wooden scraper and a rag, all the time keeping the paint fluid, filling in bits which did not work, and holding those which did. The underlying texture of leaf mould and dead twigs achieved in this way has a most convincing form. Then I began to paint in shadows here and there, with a Dalon D.77 No. 5, to 'flesh out' this background, lending depth and creating visual interest. As you look at an overall texture like this, shapes will suddenly reveal themselves to you as leaves or pieces of bark or whatever, and a fleck of shadow and a dot or two to highlight an edge will reinforce these images and make them clear to everyone. Bring out these forms as they occur to you and slowly build up the strength and quality of your backgrounds. Do not let your painting be spread evenly over the picture plane but give the viewer 'high' points to focus on. These will lead the eye over the canvas in leaps and bounds and make the picture an exciting visual experience.

I used this technique here to lead the viewer into the painting and finally to the focal point, the head of the toad. I painted the leaves of the dock next, which were an extension of the background as far as painting technique went. They were, however, raised above the surface of the ground and had to appear so. Use of shadow is invaluable and should always be considered as an integral part of the composition as well as the device which 'fixes' objects in their proper place.

The background thus completed, I started underpainting the subject of the piece – the toad. A dark green (Prussian Blue and Yellow Ochre) was painted over the area of the toad and the edges were softened into the background with the smallest Dalon fan, rendering a silhouette. Into the soft paint I began to dot in the toad's top colour (Yellow Ochre, Titanium White and Terre Verte, to give a pale grey-green) and I used the actual shape and position of these spots of paint to describe the curves and lines of the toad's body. Paint a little, then stand back and study is the rule; slowly build up the detail, the light and shade, the atmosphere of the painting as you go. The time spent achieving an image in paint is what gives it its depth of feeling, so work carefully and build slowly towards the finish of your work.

The eyes – the colour first, the black pupils second, and the highlights last – usually come at the end of the job, yet with this particular painting one crucial stage remained: the bright shaft of light that would cut right through the composition. I left the picture to go off for a day, then began carefully overpainting the strip of bright illumination with bright gold (Titanium White and Chrome Yellow) on a D.77 No. 2. Every surface facing the light source was filled in and the contours were faithfully followed. When the toad was thus overpainted, I lightened the colour with more Titanium White to separate further and enhance this, the focal point of my piece. The worm was dealt with last of all, and it was not difficult to find a model out in the garden.

Finishing a picture is a wonderfully satisfying moment. Drop your (beautifully cleaned) brush into your brush pot and sit back. Try to be another person who looks on the work for the first time and give an honest appraisal. Seeing a steady improvement in your painting is well worthwhile, and each picture finished leads you on to the next; to another chance to do better.

Fig. 67 *The Toad and the Worm*

Contrast is a useful device in wildlife painting, where the nature of your subject can be seen in comparison with objects familiar to the viewer. Temperament, scale and texture can be underlined in this way, and in the picture of the brooding robin (**fig. 69**) the rusty metal oil-lamp and the coarse wooden planking give us clear information as to the bird's size and the softness of its plumage. The broom handle and the old fishing rod suggest some of the clutter in which a robin might well feel at home, and so inform us further as to the little bird's nature. The strong shaft of sunlight, just catching the nesting bird, apart from having a strong visual effect of its own, captures that special moment when the hitherto hidden bird is suddenly seen illuminated. The very static nature of the devices around the robin and the fact that it is painted as an integral part of the still life, suggest that, although the bird is aware of being observed, it remains frozen in its situation. It is worth noting here that all substances have a surface character which must be suggested in paint. Here I have tried to paint a living bird covered in feathers; but a porcelain figure of a robin, however realistic, would still be made of porcelain and must therefore appear so in your picture.

Fig. 68

Fig. 69 *Robin*

The composition of the hedgehogs (**fig. 70**) was considered after I had seen a baby hedgehog's face and realized, first, that I had not really seen a hedgehog's face in detail before (they are usually tucked out of sight) and, second, what a delightful face it was. I used a setting of smooth roots and autumn leaves to give contrast and scale, and painted three of the creatures to give three slightly differing aspects of the face. The spines were achieved by painting the body shape in Vandyke Brown and then, using a Dalon No. 1 pencil brush, with a single stroke per spine, painting in the buff colour of the prickles into the wet oil paint.

Fig. 70 *Hedgehogs*

Do not waste time painting every perfect blade of grass unless it has a clear purpose in supporting the point of your picture. If you wish to express the wonderful diversity and brilliance of colour found in the bird world by painting a jay confronting a cock pheasant, you need no more than the merest suggestion of background, letting the riot of colour in the plumage be the sum total of the work. If, on the other hand, you wish to describe the delicacy and jewel-like quality of a tiny mouse, placing your subject against a great scaffolding of dark branches and leaves really emphasizes the exquisiteness of the mouse to your audience and makes a very clear statement of your intent. Here (**fig. 71**), the leaves also serve to hide the weasel and give it a menacing, lurking quality, further describing and contrasting the two subjects of the picture.

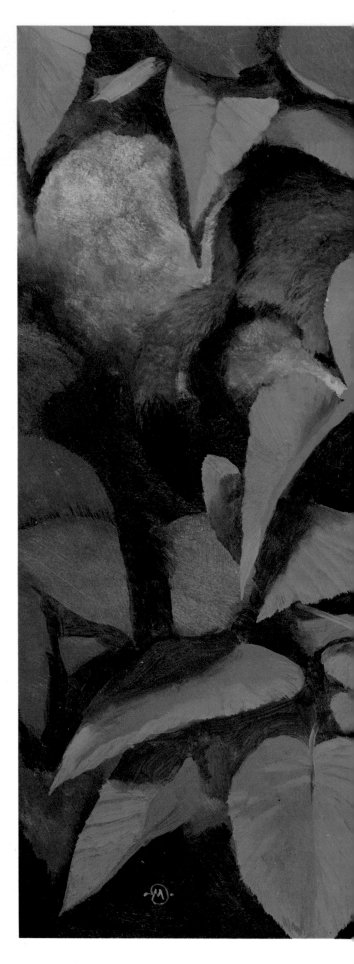

Fig. 71 *Weasel and Mouse*

Fig. 72 *Python and Prey*

A python with its prey (**fig. 72**) is a subject with a wealth of opportunities for the painter. The contours of a snake can be formed into an endless variety of shapes. They coil and intertwine, over and under, and are a wonderful visual maze for the viewer. Here I have set the snake on a sand background which suggests by colour the snake's integration with its environment. The pattern of the scales is a work of art in itself. Like a tapestry with each stitch a subtly different colour, the scales describe the beautiful forms of the creature beneath the skin. The head of the serpent is expressionless, alien, and the bird is all but lost beneath the massive power of the coils – just a hint of colour, already overwhelmed.

Using oil paint, I started with Vandyke Brown over the whole picture area and left this for three days to set dry. On this I painted with a Dalon 1 inch flat the sand colour, Yellow Ochre mixed with Zinc White, and stippled this with a Rowney bristle stippler to achieve an even colour, textured as sand. I drew in the outline of the snake with a 2H pencil and began painting in the illuminated areas of the snake's skin with the sand colour lightened with Titanium White. Each scale was achieved by a single stroke of a Dalon D.77 No. 1 brush. The shadows cast on to the sand were created by removing the overpainted sand colour to reveal the dark underpainting. This can be done with a dry brush or a rag, or with anything that will give you a satisfying result. Where the snake disturbed the sand with its coils, I used a stiff brush (a Dalon D.44 is fairly unyielding) to re-create what had happened in life. The result can be uncannily accurate. The forms of the snake were shaded by painting on the same Vandyke Brown as the underpaint and then dotting in the scales in long, lateral lines along the forms of the body. I allowed the paint to blend naturally as I moved my brush from the wet, dark paint to the slightly drier pale colour. By this stage I was using small brushes and working on very small areas. I reinforced light against dark and rough against smooth to keep all the essential forms within the piece readable and clear.

The feathers were painted with a very rough old brush (something like a No. 4) and I deliberately left the brush to give me a ruffled effect. I painted the shadows on the plumage first and then the highlights over the top. Pure Titanium White highlights to bring the serpent to life and Lamp Black with Vandyke Brown to reinforce the deepest shadow concluded the picture. After a day I softened some parts of the work with a fan. You, too, will get into the habit of looking at what you do with the overall effect in mind, changing and adapting where you feel improvement can be made as you go along.

Chris Good...
and Battersea Ar...

E V E R Y
O N E

by Jo Clifford

**This production of *Every One* was first performed at
Battersea Arts Centre on 2 March 2016**

**The play was first performed at the
Royal Lyceum Theatre, Edinburgh, on 19 March 2010**

EVERY ONE

by Jo Clifford

Cast

MARY	Angela Clerkin
JOE	Michael Fenton Stevens
MAZZ	Nicola Weston
KEVIN	Nick Finegan
MOTHER	Eileen Nicholas
MAN	Nigel Barrett

Creative Team

Director	Chris Goode
Designer	Naomi Dawson
Associate Designer	Cécile Trémolières
Lighting Designer	Katharine Williams
Production Manager	Helen Mugridge
Stage Manager	Griffyn Gilligan
Producer	Ric Watts
Critical Writer	Maddy Costa

Every One

Jo Clifford's *Every One* is the first play staged by Chris Goode & Company in its five years of existence that wasn't either written by Chris or created collectively in response to other motley texts. Why this one? Although written by a transgender woman, it presents a heteronormative family that is not only white and middle-class but repeatedly claims, without question, the privileged space of being considered 'ordinary': they're 'just normal people', they emphasise, 'like everyone'. When Jo disrupts that picture, she does so through the death of the mother, which, to echo my children's favourite catchphrase, isn't very fair. That the mother works as a tax inspector suggests another apparent universal – that taxes and death are the only two certainties – half of which doesn't apply to many low-waged people, or indeed mothers. Within the politics of the company, its desire to hear the voices of the marginalised and nonconformist, *Every One* seems to pose a series of problems.

It would be easy to read *Every One* as a sentimental play, a weepie, the more so for its basis in autobiography: the death of Jo's wife, Susie, in 2005. 'Time doesn't heal anything,' say Joe the character in *Every One* and Jo the playwright in unison: what changes is the ability to look at the wound. In writing of her wife's pain, and her own, Jo breaks the taboo surrounding death, the culture of silence, avoidance and discomfort, inviting a contemplation at once of bereavement and the inevitability of one's own demise. The loss of the mother is an ongoing theme in Chris' work (devastatingly so in *God/Head*), and I read a reckoning with his own mother's death in his decision to direct this play. At a surface level, *Every One* has the same directness as Blind Willie Johnson's blues song, 'Motherless Children': 'motherless children have a hard time when mother is dead'. That was autobiographical, too.

But the play has a complexity that renders its surface precarious and transparent as a thin sheet of ice. It begins with the family addressing the audience, as though inhabiting with them the same present moment: but that family move across time, into past and future, with a fluidity that is unnerving. We talked in the rehearsal room about 'queer time': whereas standardised storytelling, with its beginnings, middles and ends, is linear, queer writing is cyclical and multi-dimensional. I've encountered a similar theory of 'feminine writing' in the work of French post-structuralists (I had fun at university, I can tell you), and *Every One* is undoubtedly a feminist play. For two millennia, the iconography of Mary has been used to beat women into submission: Jo rejects that iconography and creates instead a Mary who is mundane and mortal, argumentative in the face of death and ultimately self-determining.

As much as *Every One* is focused on dying, it is also a play about living. Not just living on – the play doesn't simply end with death but also begins with it and journeys beyond – but living differently. It calls for a different spirituality: not the organised Christianity of a church that has 'dissipated all authority and power' through its insistence on heteronormativity and binary absolutes (good/evil, male/female), but a faith expressed in tender appreciation of the spectrum of humanity. The same spirituality surges again and again in Jo's work, most obviously in *The Gospel According to Jesus, Queen of Heaven*, a luminous sermon that retells stories from the Bible from a queer perspective.

Where that queered spirituality leads is to a robust resistance of capitalism. *Every One* is disgusted and incensed at the damage inflicted by capitalism. This is a play in which death claims responsibility for all the ills of the world: war, genocide and – his 'masterstroke' – an economic system that kills those it benefits as much as those it crushes. But he does so in the body of a man.

Capitalist patriarchy is destroying us, and so we need to change: to care for each other, help each other, ask 'how are you?' and really listen to the answer. The congregating we do in theatre might just be central to this shift. In 2013, Chris and Jo shared the stage at the Bike Shed in Exeter for a conversation; I sat in the audience electrified by the passion that erupted from Jo as she spoke of theatre as a place of resistance, in which people deny the 'capital-intensive economy that ... is obsessed with the notion of the individual, in competition with our fellow human beings', by working together, trusting each other and exercising empathy. Jo went on: 'If there's one quality that we need more than any other in this terrible world it is empathy. We have to resist this horrible tendency to dehumanise our fellow humans and judge them and belittle them and exploit them; we have to learn to love each other, and that's what theatre is about.' It's what *Every One* is about. It's what Chris Goode & Company is about. Jo's marginalised, nonconformist voice sings out in this play, and that's why the company is so proud to present it.

Maddy Costa
February 2016

The Company

Nigel Barrett | MAN

Nigel Barrett is an actor and theatremaker. He is a member of the Shunt collective, an Associate Artist of the New Wolsey and makes shows with Louise Mari (www.nigelandlouise.com). Recent work includes: *The Body* (Barbican Centre, Winner of the Oxford Samuel Beckett Theatre Trust Award); *The Letters of Pliny* (Radio 4); *Monument* (Trafalgar Square); *The Liberty Cap* (Radio 4); *Ur* (Festival des Ecrivains du Monde, Paris); *Be Bees* (Queen Elizabeth Olympic Park); *Mad Man* (Drum, Plymouth); *Margate/Dreamland* (National Theatre Studio/Tom Thumb Margate); *Cyrano de Bergerac* (Northern Stage/Royal & Derngate); *Basement Grotto* (Shoreditch Town Hall); *Praxis Makes Perfect* (National Theatre Wales/Berliner Festspiele); *The Boy Who Climbed Out of His Face* (Shunt); *Richard III: An Arab Tragedy* (RSC/Bouffes du Nord/BAM); *Doctors, Casualty, The Lens* (BBC); *The Passion* (National Theatre Wales); *England My England* (Channel 4) and *Pericles* (Regent's Park Open Air).

Angela Clerkin | MARY

Angela is an Associate Artist with Improbable and Chris Goode & Company. Recent theatre includes: *The Haunting of Hill House* (Liverpool Playhouse/Sonia Friedman Productions); *Early Days of a Better Nation* (Coney/UK tour); *The Bear* (Clerkinworks/Improbable/UK tour); *Monkey Bars* (Fringe First winner, Chris Goode & Company/Traverse/UK tour) and *Panic* (Improbable/Barbican/Sydney Opera House/UK tour). Other work includes: Improbable's *Lifegame* (National Theatre/UK tour/New York/Brisbane); *The Bloody Chamber, Kaput* (Northern Stage); *The Maids, Turn of the Screw* (Young Vic); Great Expectations (Welsh tour); *Season's Greetings* (Liverpool Playhouse); *Cinderella* (Lyric Hammersmith); *Habeus Corpus* (Northampton); *The Dream Killers* (BAC); *The School for Wives, Metamorphosis* (Manchester); *Shadow of a Gunman, East* (Leicester); *The Government Inspector* (WYP); *A Flea in Her Ear* (Old Vic); *Gaudete* (Almeida). TV includes: *Dr Who, Humans, Holby City, EastEnders, Dalziel & Pascoe, My Family, Sugar Rush, The Office* (series 1) and *Dean Spanley*. clerkinworks.com

Jo Clifford | Writer

Jo Clifford is a playwright and performer who lives in Edinburgh. She is the author of about eighty plays, many of which have been performed all over the world. These include: *Losing Venice, Every One, Faust* and *The Tree of Knowledge*. Her *Great Expectations* makes her the first openly transgendered woman playwright to have had a play on in London's West End. She revived her *Gospel According to Jesus Queen of Heaven* for the 2014 and 2015 Fringe, and this year takes the show to Queer Contact in Manchester and FIT in Belo Horizonte, Brazil. She is an Associate Artist with Chris Goode & Company and performed in *The Albemarle Sketchbook*. She is currently co-writing a play with Chris for the National Theatre of Scotland, which she will perform late in 2016. She is a proud father and grandmother. More info & her blog on www.teatrodomundo.com and @jocliffordplays.

Maddy Costa | Critical Writer

Maddy Costa is critical writer with Chris Goode & Company, and a freelance writer specialising in theatre, music and an ongoing disruption of 'criticism' as a practice. With Dialogue, the organisation she co-founded in 2012, she opens up space for conversation between people who make, watch and write about theatre, and co-hosts a pop-up theatre club, modelled on the book group. As associate artist with Something Other, she co-curates a website and performance night which play with possible relationships between live arts and written texts. The theatremakers and companies with whom she has worked – as critical friend, dramaturg, or shaping creative documentation – including Fuel, Coney, In Between Time, Derelict, Harry Giles, Sheila Ghelani, Leo Kay and Selina Thompson. She is a board member for Uninvited Guests, reviews for the *Guardian* and *Exeunt*, dances with the Actionettes, and keeps a blog, Deliq.

Naomi Dawson | Designer

Naomi Dawson trained at Wimbledon School of Art and Kunstacademie, Maastricht. Recent theatre design includes: *Doctor Faustus* (RSC); *Beryl* (Rose, Kingston); *Brave New World* (Northampton/UK tour); *Weaklings* (Warwick Arts/UK tour); *Men in the Cities* (Royal Court and UK tour). Other theatre design includes: *Hotel, Three More Sleepless Nights* (NT); *The White Devil, The Roaring Girl, As You Like It, King John* (RSC); *Beryl* (West Yorkshire Playhouse/UK tour); *Care* (Watford Palace); *Kasimir and Karoline, Fanny and Alexander, Love and Money* (Malmo Stadsteater); *Wildefire, Belongings, The Gods Weep* (Hampstead); *Men in the Cities* (Traverse); *Dancing at Lughnasa, In Praise of Love* (Theatre Royal, Northampton); *Monkey Bars* (Unicorn/Traverse); *Landscape and Monologue* (Ustinov, Bath); *Amerika, Krieg der Bilder* (Staatstheater

Mainz); *Scorched* (Old Vic Tunnels); *Mary Shelley, The Glass Menagerie, Speechless* (Shared Experience); *The Typist* (Sky Arts); *The Container, Phaedra's Love, The Pope's Wedding, Forest of Thorns* (Young Vic); *King Pelican, Speed Death of the Radiant Child* (Drum, Plymouth); *If That's All There Is* (Lyric); *State of Emergency, Mariana Pineda* (Gate); *...SISTERS* (Gate/Headlong); *Stallerhof, Richard III, The Cherry Orchard, Summer Begins* (Southwark Playhouse); *Attempts on Her Life, Widows, Touched* (BAC); *Home, In Blood, Venezuela, Mud, Trash* (Arcola). Opera design includes: *Madama Butterfly, The Lottery, The Fairy Queen* (Bury Court Opera); *Madama Butterfly* (Arcola)

Michael Fenton Stevens | JOE

Theatre includes: *Love for Love, Queen Anne* (RSC 2015); *Stand* (Chris Goode & Company); *Yes, Prime Minister, The Bed Before Yesterday, Scissor Happy, Fields of Ambrosia, It's a Wonderful Life, The Importance of Being Ernest, Amadeus, Colombe, The Country Wife, An English Tragedy, The Tempest, St Joan,* and numerous Pantomime Dames. TV includes: *New Tricks, Ballot Monkeys, Benidorm, Outnumbered, Mrs Biggs, Not Going Out, My Family, Nighty Night, Lead Balloon, Persuassion, Absolute Power, Coronation Street, Look Around You, Footballers' Wives, Trevor's World of Sport, Mr Bean, Only Fools and Horses, One Foot in the Grave, As Time Goes By, My Hero, People Like Us, The Legacy of Reginald Perrin, KYTV* (Golden Rose Winner); *Holby City, EastEnders, Doctors, Spitting Image* (including a no.1 hit singing 'The Chicken Song'). Radio includes: *The Archers, Old Harry's Game, Radio Active, Inspector Steine, Dirk Gently's Holistic Detective Agency, The Hitchhiker's Guide to the Galaxy, Rapid Eye Movement,* and many plays and readings). Member of the comedy pop parody group The HeeBeeGeeBees and the voice of Mr Beakman in the childrens' cartoon series, *3rd & Bird.*

Griffyn Gilligan | Stage Manager

Training: Royal Central School of Speech and Drama, MA in Advanced Theatre Practice. Theatre includes: Jaq in *Teddy Ferrara* at the Donmar Warehouse; member of the ensemble Ponyboy Curtis. Griffyn has stage managed several American productions and festivals, but *Every One* marks his London debut.

Chris Goode | Director

Chris Goode is a writer, director, performer and musician. He has been lead artist of Chris Goode & Company since its inception in 2011. He is also director of the performance ensemble Ponyboy Curtis. Recent work includes, for Chris Goode & Company: *Weaklings* (Warwick Arts Centre); *Men in the Cities* (Royal Court/Traverse); *STAND* (Oxford

Playhouse); *Longwave* (Shoreditch Town Hall); *The Forest & The Field, GOD/HEAD* (Ovalhouse); *9* (West Yorkshire Playhouse); *Monkey Bars* (Unicorn/Traverse); *The Adventures of Wound Man and Shirley* (BAC). As an independent maker: *Apathy* (Theatre Uncut); *Ponyboy Curtis at the Yard* (The Yard); *MAD MAN* (Drum, Plymouth); *The Worst of Scottee* (Roundhouse); *Infinite Lives* (Tobacco Factory); *The Loss of All Things* (as part of *66 Books* at the Bush); *Who You Are* (Tate Modern); *Glass House* (Royal Opera House Covent Garden); *Landscape and Monologue* (Ustinov, Bath); *King Pelican* (Drum, Plymouth); *...SISTERS* (Headlong/Gate). Chris is the author of *The Forest and the Field: Changing Theatre in a Changing World* (Oberon), and he hosts the Chris Goode & Company podcast, Thompson's Live.

Nick Finegan | KEVIN

Nick Finegan is a London-based actor and theatre maker. He studied English and Drama at the University of Bristol. Theatre includes: *Weaklings* (Chris Goode & Company/Warwick Arts Centre); *Ponyboy Curtis* (Chris Goode & Company/The Yard); *Richard II, Titus Andronicus* (Malachite); *Arcadia, As You Like It, Two Gentlemen of Verona* (Shakespeare at the Tobacco Factory); *Coram Boy* (Melly Still); *Men* (Bristol Old Vic Studio); *Waiting For Alice, The Country* (Pleasance); *Believer's Anonymous* (Holly Roughan/Cordelia Lynn); *Paradise Project* (Emma Stirling). Film includes: *Mujica* (Ken McMullen); *Pulse* (Misha Vertkin); *Lie Still* (Sean Hogan).

Helen Mugridge | Production Manager

Helen is an experienced stage and production manager. Her previous work includes: *Stowaway, Analogue* (national tour); *Golem, 1927* (UK and international tour); *Stand* (Chris Goode & Company/Oxford Playhouse); *Re-Enactments* (Analogue, Shoreditch Town Hall); *Mess* (Caroline Horton, national tour); *The Secret Agent* (Theatre O/Edinburgh/Young Vic/national tour); *The Victorian in the Wall* (Will Adamsdale, Royal Court/national tour); *Monkey Bars* (Chris Goode & Company, Edinburgh/UK tour/Unicorn); *Mass Observation, Inspector Sands* (Almeida); *Cooking Ghosts* (Beady Eye/south-east tour/Camden People's Theatre); *Penumbra, BYO, Thickskin* (research and development); *2401 Objects* (Analogue, National Theatre and European development/Edinburgh 2011/national and European tour); *The Adventures of Wound Man and Shirley* (Chris Goode & Company, Edinburgh 2011); *Total Football* (Ridiculusmus, Barbican Pit/Belfast Festival/autumn 2012 tour); *Beachy Head* (Analogue, national and European tour); *Everything Must Go* (Beady Eye/Kristin Fredrickson, national and European tour).

Eileen Nicholas | MOTHER

Theatre includes: *The Scar Test* (Untold Theatre); *It's Only Words* (Oràn Mór); *I Killed Rasputin* (George Square); *All About My Mother* (Old Vic); *The Queen of Lucky People* (Traverse); *Buried Child* (Upstairs at the Gatehouse); *I Didn't Always Live Here* (Finborough); *Lobster/Vantastic* (Ovalhouse); *Misery* (Edinburgh Festival); *Elizabeth Gordon Quinn, Through the Leaves* (Traverse/Bush); *Same Old Moon* (Gielgud); *Juno and the Paycock* (Royal Lyceum); *American Bagpipes* (Royal Court/Royal Exchange, Manchester); *Endgame, Request Programme* (Donmar Warehouse); *The Revenger's Tragedy* (Cambridge Theatre Co); *A Lady of Letters* (Theatre Royal, Bury St Edmunds). Awarded the Fringe First and Time Out London Theatre Award for *Request Programme*. TV includes: *Midwinter of the Spirit* (ITV); *Law and Order UK, Half Broken Things, Taggart, Between the Lines, The Bill, Casualty, Dr Findley's Casebook, Doctors, The Final Run, Mitch*. Film includes: *Gunned Down, Falcon, Mind The Gap, Blackwood, The Quiet Ones, January, The Wee Man, Late Bloomers, Bomber* (Best Actress, Bend Film Festival, Oregon; Best Actress, Nashville Film Festival; Best Supporting Actress, Kiev International Festival); *Trainspotting, Regeneration, Mr Corbett's Ghost, Widowmaker, Hush* (short); *The Lump* (short).

Cécile Trémolières | Associate Designer

Born in Paris, Cécile trained in Wimbledon College of Art, graduating with a first-class degree in June 2013. Cécile was a finalist of the Linbury Prize for Stage Design 2013 and nominated Best Set Designer by the Off West End Theatre Awards 2014. Cécile's work has been exhibited at the Prague Quadrennial 2015, and at the V&A exhibition *Make/Believe: UK Design for Performance 2011–2015*. Work includes: *My People*, directed by Aled Pedrick and Steffan Donnelly (Clywd); *Impermanent Theatre*, with Impermanence Dance Theatre (touring UK); *Invisible Treasure*, devised by fanSHEN (Ovalhouse); *Piranha Heights*, directed by Max Barton (Old Red Lion); *The Mikvah Project*, directed by Jay Miller (The Yard) and *Harajuku Girls*, directed by Jude Christian (Finborough).

Ric Watts | Producer

Ric is Producer and Co-Founder of Chris Goode & Company, for whom he has produced all of the company's work including *Men in the Cities, Weaklings, STAND, Monkey Bars, GOD/HEAD* and *The Adventures of Wound Man and Shirley*. He is also Executive Producer for Unlimited Theatre (*The Giant & The Bear, MONEY the game show, The Noise, Play Dough* and *Am I Dead Yet?*); Producer for Analogue (*Mile End, Beachy Head, 2401 Objects, Re-enactments, Transports, Stowaway*); and

Executive Producer for the newly independent Leeds-based international festival Transform. He also sits on the board of Cartoon de Salvo; on the advisory board for RashDash; and the Large Grants committee at Wellcome Trust; as well as regularly mentoring emerging artists and producers in the North of England. Ric has previously produced for Cartoon de Salvo, Ridiculusmus, Kazuko Hohki, theimaginarybody, The TEAM, Filter and Schtanhaus, The Frequency D'ici, Laura Mugridge, Royal & Derngate, The Other Way Works, Slung Low, Queer Up North International Festival and Hannah Jane Walker and Chris Thorpe.

Nicola Weston | MAZZ

Nicola Weston trained at Italia Conti and received her MA in Performance Making from Goldsmiths, University of London. She is an actor, theatremaker and community arts practitioner from south-east London. Theatre includes: *Topcat* (Wimbledon) and *Located in Transit* (The Yard). Television includes: *The Bill*.

Katharine Williams | Lighting Designer

Katharine Williams is a lighting designer for live performance. She works in the UK and internationally. Her designs have been seen in China, Hong Kong, New Zealand, Canada, the USA, Mexico, Ireland, Holland, Spain, Italy, Germany, Armenia, Romania, Russia and the Czech Republic. For Chris Goode & Company she has designed *Weaklings, Men in the Cities* and *GOD/HEAD*. As a filmmaker, she is currently collaborating with Clare Duffy on Extreme Light North. Katharine is lead artist on the *Love Letters to the Home Office* project which campaigns using art, words and theatre to stop the means-tested tiering of Human Rights that is currently in place in the UK for international families. She is the founder of the Crew for Calais initiative.

 Chris
Goode
&Co.

Chris Goode & Company is a collaboration between lead artist Chris Goode, producer Ric Watts, writer and critic Maddy Costa and a fluid ensemble of makers, designers and performers. At the heart of the enemble is a core group of associate artists with whom we work more frequently – Angela Clerkin, Jo Clifford, Wendy Hubbard, James Lewis, Pauline Mayers and Jamie Wood.

Chris Goode & Company make theatre by creating welcoming spaces and interesting structures for unexpected things to happen in. We tell stories in ways that are both experimental and at the same time accessible and inclusive, and think out loud about who we all are, hoping to catch a glimpse of how we might live better together.

Our principal aim is to make space for unheard voices. This is done by:

- Talking to people about their lives, and using their words to make their work

- Involving people in the imagining and making of their work who maybe don't think of themselves as artists

- Recovering and presenting lost or neglected work by artists (both historical and contemporary) whose lives and thoughts have led them to be marginalised or overlooked

- And creating bold original work that represents queer, dissident, and politically nonconformist perspectives

Since forming in 2011, Chris Goode & Company has created an award-winning body of work that includes *Every One* (Battersea Arts Centre), *Weaklings* (Warwick Arts Centre and touring), *Men in the Cities* (Royal Court, Traverse Theatre and touring), *STAND* (Oxford Playhouse, Battersea Arts Centre and touring), *Longwave* (house Recommission), *Monkey Bars* (Unicorn Theatre, Traverse Theatre and touring), *9* (West Yorkshire Playhouse), *The Forest & The Field* (Ovalhouse) and touring, *GOD/HEAD* (Ovalhouse and Theatre in the Mill), *The Adventures of Wound Man & Shirley* (Edinburgh, BAC and touring), *Where We Meet* (Edinburgh), *Keep Breathing* (Drum Theatre Plymouth) and various editions of *Open House* (West Yorkshire Playhouse, Mayfest, National Theatre Studio, Ovalhouse).

www.chrisgoodeandcompany.co.uk

BATTERSEA ARTS CENTRE

Battersea Arts Centre is based in a beautiful old town hall where people come together to be creative, see a show, explore local heritage, visit the Scratch Bar, play or relax.

Battersea Arts Centre invites people in to watch early versions of shows, to hear their feedback. They call this Scratch. Finished shows can use any room in the building, from the attic to the artists' bedrooms to the Council Chamber.

Battersea Arts Centre is open all day for anyone to explore. Children and adults can play together in their indoor playspace, The Bees Knees or enjoy monthly fun-filled Family Saturdays. Young people join activities after school to develop their creativity, confidence and enterprising ideas. Battersea Arts Centre also celebrates the rich heritage of their building and the local area through events and discussions.

All of this helps them achieve their mission 'to inspire people, to take creative risks, to shape the future.'

For those who can't make it to Battersea, they also take their shows across the UK and the world. Scratch has been adopted as far afield as Sydney and New York and Battersea Arts Centre has successfully sparked new approaches to creativity across the globe.

- Welcomes over 100,000 people to its building every year
- Inspires the local community to get creative with around 5000 young people and children participating in workshops yearly
- Works with over 400 artists to put on over 650 performances and tour at least 12 shows and projects each year

bac.org.uk | @battersea_arts

EVERY ONE

Jo Clifford

To Susie,
dear loved one
for the last time

'*Things unattempted yet in prose or rhyme.*'
John Milton, *Paradise Lost*

'*A condition of complete simplicity*
Costing not less than everything.'
T.S. Eliot, *Four Quartets*

Before You Start to Read

Where the play comes from

At the end of the first performance of my *Anna Karenina*, one of my lovely daughters said to me: 'Dad! That was about us! You put us up there!'

She was right, even though I hadn't intended that, and obviously the characters she had just seen were originally nominally Tolstoy's. It's as if everything that happens to me forms part of a kind of storehouse from which, sometimes consciously and sometimes not, I draw my characters.

This play is unusual for me because it comes very directly from a recent memory. Which I will describe soon.

It's only really in the last few weeks, as I have been reflecting on what I need to tell the actors before rehearsals (which, as I write this, begin tomorrow), that another memory has come back into consciousness. One I know has given this play its first impetus and final shape.

When I was twelve years old, my mother came to see me in the boarding school in which I had been put. Such visits were unusual, partly because she lived so very far away, and partly too because there was a sense that it was somehow 'good for boys' to be separated from our parents. Especially our mothers.

She took me out one Sunday that November, and then – joy of joys – I saw her again on the Wednesday. We were all to watch a rugby match; and she came along too. She brought along my little dog, Sally. Sally was a Jack Russell terrier and I loved carrying her inside my jumper so she could stick her neck out at the collar.

We were due to meet again the next day, the Thursday, when she was to be at my confirmation service in the school chapel. This was a rite of passage service where we reaffirmed our baptismal vows and were then allowed to take communion.

Part of the service consisted of each of us going up to the Bishop and kneeling before him. He was to lay his hands on our heads and say a blessing. My mum wrote me a letter, which I had received that morning, to say that I wasn't to worry if I didn't feel anything when this happened. When she was confirmed she had been eagerly anticipating some profound experience at this moment and was very disappointed when apparently nothing happened.

Whatever I felt at the moment, she wanted to reassure me, it would all be fine.

I was unexpectedly called away by the assistant headteacher, and off I went, with the letter still in my pocket, to be told by my grieving father that my mother had died very suddenly in the night.

It was a brain haemorrhage. It came out of nowhere. It devastated my young life.

Death is like that. I did not know it when I wrote this play, but I understand now that this experience was the seed that first generated it.

Consciously, however, this play came from the death of my wife, Susie, in February 2005.

The process began in May or June 2004, when she suffered from something that was diagnosed as a stroke. Out of nowhere, she said she felt some evil creature fixing itself to her shoulder and battening on to her. For a while she could not move; then she was taken to hospital.

I was away at the time, and could not help her.

She seemed to be on the road to recovery; but in August that year she started to lose her peripheral vision, become disorientated, and suffered from the most agonising headaches. Again she fell unconscious, again she was taken to hospital; but this time they found a brain tumour. They drilled a hole in the back of her head, located the tumour, analysed it; and discovered it was extremely malignant, and too close to the brain stem to be surgically removed.

They told me she might last for a week or so, but most likely she would die within days.

As it turned out, she lived another six months.

I cannot yet write about that time.

Afterwards, I became aware of how incompetent our culture is when it comes to the universal fact of death. It was almost impossible for me to talk about my experience; and there was a conspicuous lack of public events, either in the church, or the theatre, or anywhere, that helped me understand what had happened or which could help me continue to live with it.

A dear old friend of mine, the actor Suzanne Dance, had at about the same time suffered the death of her mother, and she was having a similar experience. We decided to try to pool our talents to see what could be done. The result is *Leave to Remain*, a ritualistic theatre event with words and music played live on the cello, which we have performed about two or three times a year ever since.

Leave to Remain is designed to be mostly performed in non-theatre spaces; *Every One* is an attempt to use the wonderful, amazing communication resources offered by a beautiful theatre like Edinburgh's Royal Lyceum.

Both pieces are an attempt to break the taboo surrounding death and offer a way forward in the face of it.

I became very ill in the year following Susie's death. The mitral valve in my heart was no longer functioning properly and had to be repaired. My heart was literally broken and bleeding.

In the operation, my heart had to be stopped for the surgeon to repair it.

In that sense, I, too, have died.

Certainly I had to face the possibility of my own death; both before the operation and after it, when miscommunication resulted in my being seriously overdosed with warfarin and being close to bleeding to death.

Even now, each time I become aware of my own heart beating I also become aware that one day, and perhaps now, it will stop.

This sense is intensified by the fact that I have just reached the age of sixty. This feels to me like a good time to contemplate the inevitable fact of my coming death.

Recently my mother-in-law's health has deteriorated. I ring her up every morning; each time I hear her phone ring I know one morning she may have left us in the night and so not be there to answer it.

I have a dear friend, too, who suffers from incurable kidney disease. There is a possibility she may die suddenly at night. She lives alone, and was tormented by her thought of her dead body lying for days before someone discovered it. So we agreed she would text me every morning just to let us both know she is still alive.

This closeness to death does not depress or frighten me. On the contrary, it seems to heighten my appreciation of life.

This, too, I wish to communicate.

Everyman

As is well known, *Everyman* is a celebrated example of a late-medieval mystery play. It was written towards the end of the fifteenth century and presents the drama of human life and death in allegorical form.

My first intention had been to adapt it; but in the end it became clear that the play was too deeply entwined in an aspect of the Christian tradition that is now defunct; and that this would make it impossible for it to be successfully staged.

It is a very wonderful work: I admire its uncompromising insistence that we will all die, and need to use that awareness to inform our lives.

What happens in *Everyman* is summarised by the Man at the end of Act One.

I would commend the text, which can be found online at:
http://www.luminarium.org/medlit/everyman.htm

The character of the 'Mother' and the 'Man'

In one of the crises of her final illness, Susie became aware of the presence of her dead father. She experienced him as being present as vividly as I was, I think, and she knew he was there to help her.

She also knew he was in another dimension. This dimension was as real as the dimension she was at present inhabiting, along with the rest of us, but the difficulty was that the two dimensions were out of alignment. She knew she had to get them into alignment, somehow, and felt that was the task she had to fulfil.

On my way home to write this piece, I happened to meet someone I am very fond of but had lost touch with.

The reason we had not met each other for a while is that she has been very ill with cancer. She has had to have three tumours removed; and on the last occasion, just before Christmas, they had operated on her intestines with the expectation that the tumour was inoperable.

However, to everyone's delight and surprise, the surgeon discovered that the tumour, although very large, could in fact be removed and she has now been declared free of cancer.

She told me that while she was recovering from the operation she was lying on her back in pain and had a sudden vision that told her that the 'afterlife' does not happen after our lives but is happening here and now: and that the two worlds are utterly intertwined.

We have access to this 'other world' in our dreams, in drug-induced hallucinations, or in moments of the intensest sexual pleasure. I enter it each time I create.

Among other occasions.

When I was seventeen I found myself working in a geriatric ward with severely demented patients. Although to the outward eye they often seem to be in some kind of vegetative state, it seemed clear to me then they lived an intense inner life. Recent research with Alzheimer's patients indicates that the key to their successful treatment seems to lie, not in forcibly trying to make their inner state conform to what we call 'normality', but in us respecting their world and accommodating it.

This 'other world' has been given many names. Jung called aspects of it 'the collective unconscious'. A recent visit to Auschwitz confirmed that just as individuals tend to bury their traumas in the individual subconscious, so have we in Europe buried our collective trauma, the Holocaust, in the collective subconscious.

Death obviously belongs to this realm. The last time he made his appearance most forcefully felt was at the convulsive transition from the Middle Ages to the Renaissance. We are deep in the middle of another convulsive transition: and this is one reason we need to pay attention to him now.

When we use the word 'death' we think we understand what we are talking about. But in fact, He is a mystery. We should keep our minds open: and that is why he is not called 'Death' in *Every One* but instead, more openly and simply, 'Man'.

He could, of course, as easily be a woman; and that is how I portrayed Death the last time I attempted to do so, in my *Inés de Castro*.

But in this play it is important s/he is portrayed as male.

It is, of course, perhaps a rash undertaking to try to dramatise this world at all. But I consider it worth attempting.

Staging

I like to think of my plays as gifts. Gifts for all the other professionals involved. Or perhaps better as invitations. Invitations to display their skills, creativity and talents.

And here on the page, the script is an invitation to you. To imagine...

So I hesitate, always, to prescribe stage directions; and in any case I have only limited capacity to visualise. I focus on the feeling, and I try to find the right words.

I understand, however, that it might help the reader if I gave a little clue as to how this play looked in its first incarnation.

Francis O'Connor's beautiful design consisted essentially of a moving perspex screen that, when light was shone on it, became a mirror; and when light was shone behind it became translucent.

At the beginning of the play it filled the space under the proscenium arch so the audience were reflected in it as they entered. As the play begins, it retreated upstage and formed a neutral backdrop for the family members. They each had their little space, a kind of spotlit home from which they could speak directly to the audience or turn and speak to each other.

When Mary entered hospital, there was a dummy of her placed in a hospital bed that the audience could see behind the screen, with the family gathered round it. Mary and the Man interacted in front of the screen.

In Act Two, the configuration changed as she moved into the empty dark space of Death's hinterland.

As the family reasserted its presence into the world, it was clear something had irrevocably changed: Mary's light may still have been there, but she was no longer in it.

After the child appeared on the swing, and went, at the very end, the most beautiful tree appeared behind the screen upstage.

This helped move the play towards a tentative sense of hope.

Finally...

At the risk of sounding obvious: this play is designed to give pleasure to both performer and audience. It is not designed to sit on a page. If a speech or scene does not seem meaningful to you, read it aloud.

Or better still: read it to a friend.

Author's Note

Thanks to Katie Innes, Rebecca Innes, Marie Lamont and Claire Lewis for inspiration and encouragement.

Just as this script was going to press, I heard of the death of Rolando Toro Arañeda. He has helped me immeasurably in the last years, and I wish to dedicate it to his memory.

J.C.
2010

Quick Note for the New Edition

It makes me so happy that dear Nick Hern Books are re-publishing this text to coincide with Chris Goode's new production.

Chris Goode is one of the very finest theatre artists working in Britain just now, and he has assembled the most fantastic creative team.

The old Council Chamber in Battersea Arts Centre, where the show is being performed, is a stunningly beautiful space. I have rewritten Joe's speech on page 21 in its honour. Those wishing to perform in a theatre that looks very different will need to consult the author via the publisher to devise an appropriate replacement for this speech.

Otherwise the script is mostly unchanged.

J.C.
2016

Every One was first performed at the Royal Lyceum Theatre, Edinburgh, on 19 March 2010, with the following cast:

MARY	Kathryn Howden
JOE	Jonathan Hackett
MAZZ	Jenny Hulse
KEVIN	Kyle McPhail
MOTHER	Tina Gray
MAN	Liam Brennan
CHILD	Jenny Hulse
DANCERS	Courtney Bladen, Olivia Barnett Brown, Natalie Craigie, Monette O'Hara, Elaine Anderson, Elaine Farris, Mary Matthews, Kathryn Wilkinson, Hannah Titlestad, Margaret Anderson, Kathleen A. Krievs, Katrina Stimson

Director	Mark Thomson
Designer	Francis O'Connor
Lighting Designer	Davy Cunningham
Composer	Philip Pinsky
Choreographer	Rhiana Laws

Characters

MARY

JOE, *her husband*

MAZZ, *their daughter*

KEVIN, *their son*

Mary's MOTHER

MAN

Also a CHILD *and* DANCERS

ACT ONE

The family come onstage. MARY, JOE, MAZZ, KEVIN *and the* MOTHER. *The* MOTHER *is in a wheelchair. Each go to their own space. And then there is a pause.*

JOE	You first.
MARY	Why me?
JOE	It's your play.
MARY	I suppose it is.
JOE	You always said –
MARY	Women should be more at the centre of things. I know.
JOE	Here you are then.
MARY	Yes. Well. I'm... I'm... Well it's hard to say, isn't it, hard to explain who you are. What would you say? I'll say... I'll just stick to the facts. My name is Mary Jane Hunter Spring. Hunter's my husband's name but I didn't want to lose my own. So when we got married I just kind of tacked it on. And it's a wee bit double-barrelled and pompous but I like it. And... I live with my husband, Joe, short for Joseph, which he hates, so it's easy to wind him up if I need to, and he's a teacher and we have two children: Mazz who's just left school, and wants to be a fashion designer,

       and Kev who's about to go into sixth form
       and spends his whole life on the computer.
And we live in an ordinary kind of house. And it's
       a bit messy.
We're just normal people, really. So I don't know
       what all the fuss is about.
And, well, I work as a tax inspector. Which isn't
       all that normal I suppose.
For some reason our friends find it hilarious.
Watch out here's the tax inspector.
Better stash the money away.
How about hiding it under the mattress?
No, I don't find it very funny either.
They let me work part time, which is great. And
       I'm good at numbers, which is great too. And
       the job stretches me a bit so I'm not brain-
       dead at the end of the day and at the same
       time it's not too taxing.
Look, I've made a joke.
What I mean is I don't want one of those jobs that
       takes over your whole life.
I've better things to do with my time.
And that's it.
Joe! Your turn.

JOE   I'm Joe. I used to teach Latin.
Amo amas amat
Mensa o mensa mensam mensae mensae
Oh table I could say in Latin
Oh table please be good and support my food.
And I liked that.
I liked being able to talk to tables.
And chairs and floors and trees and the world
       in general.
Latin's a good place to be.
It's an ordered world. A kind of refuge.
And you go into it out of the chaos and come
       out... refreshed.
And maybe understanding a bit more about your
       own language and your world as well.
I liked teaching Latin. My pupils liked it too.

> But then they stopped us teaching Latin
> And I taught Classical Studies instead.
> That was okay. A bit watery.
> Kind of Latin watered down.
> But then they stopped that too.
> Said it wasn't relevant.
> Scumbags. As if being relevant had anything to do
>   with anything.
> Morons.
> So then they tried to make me teach computing.
> Ones and zeroes. Heap of shit.
> So I switched to Modern Studies. And I like that.
>   Mostly.
> Kids need to understand.
> Need to understand something about the world.
> Knowledge is power, I think.
> And jokes are good for the soul.
> I believe that.

> *Pause.*

MARY   I'd say we were happy.

JOE   I'd say that too.

MARY   Can't think why.

JOE   It is a bit of a mystery

MARY   But there it is. More or less. I mean we have rows
        sometimes like everyone.

JOE   And then we hate each other.

MARY   But not for long.

JOE   No. Not for long.

MARY   We do our best.

> And we both worry about Kev and Mazz
> And they and Joe really get up my nose sometimes
>   but mostly we get on pretty well.
> We're in debt, of course, like everyone is, and things
>   are pretty tight, but that's true for everybody.
> And that's just how it is.

	Things keep going up.
	And another thing.
	We're still together. After thirty years!
	People look at us in amazement.
	They wonder what our secret is.

JOE   They think: we must have a skeleton in the
            cupboard somewhere.

MARY   When we don't even have enough cupboards. And
            that's a fact.

JOE   Most people are just so bloody miserable.

MARY   And what's happened? What's happened to the
            world to make this true?

JOE   We're all so rich. And the poor so poor.
            Most of the rest of the world on the breadline.
            So we can be rich. Rich and miserable!
            We should be happy.
            That's the least we could do!

MARY   That's him. He worries about things.
            As for me, I didn't set out to be normal but I
                suppose I am.
            I'm not that special.
            I'm not at all sure why I'm up here.
            It could just as well be any of you.
            And there's nothing that happens to me that
                doesn't happen to everybody.

JOE   So there's us two and our daughter Mazz and her
            brother Kev.

MARY   And we love them.

JOE   As you do, getting utterly furious with them from
            time to time.

MARY   And then there's my mum.

        And we see her.

JOE   The bane of our lives.

MARY   Oh, don't say that.

JOE   It's true.
               Look at her. She sits and sits and the only thing
                    she does
               Is make your life a misery.
               And when she was in her right mind she still made
                    your life a misery. Being judgemental all the
                    time.
               Old-school Christianity.
               The kind that forgets the bit that says Judge not
               And instead just judges all the time.
               The kind of Christianity that's way outlived its
                    usefulness
               And is slowly on its way to death.

MARY   Joe.

JOE   Yes.

MARY   Shut up!

               After a silence, the MOTHER *suddenly comes to
               life.*

MOTHER   Now I have to talk out of character or you'll never
                    understand me at all. You'll just think I'm
                    brain-dead.
               But I'm not. I'm alive.
               I'm more alive than I ever was.
               Probably more alive than the whole lot of you.
               It's just I can't quite seem able to put it into words.
               And why should I bother?
               No one listens anyway.

MARY   You see, Mum just sits.
               And I feel guilty.
               I don't understand what keeps her going.

MOTHER   I sometimes wonder what keeps me alive.
               They do give me a lot of pills.
               It's amazing what the doctors can do nowadays.

JOE   Another thing I just don't understand.
               Why we devote so much time and energy and
                    effort to prolonging our lives

                    When all we do with all those extra years of life
                    Is spend them locked up in a home.

MARY   Well we can't kill them.
                    That's how the Nazis started.

JOE   That's true. Still, if I go demented, kill me.

MOTHER   Speak for yourself.
                    And why should I have to die just to save you
                          trouble?

JOE   It's not about that!

MOTHER   I just make you uncomfortable. So you want me to
                          go away.
                    Well I'm not going to.

JOE   You must admit you don't look as if you live a
                          happy life.

MOTHER   What do you know about it?
                    Just because I sit and drool.
                    Maybe it's quite fun to sit and drool.

JOE   Well is it?

MOTHER   I'm too doped-up to notice.
                    But it's better than standing up in front of a
                          classroom full of bored schoolkids and trying
                          to teach them.
                    Better than sitting in an office processing tax
                          returns.
                    It's… restful. That's what it is. Restful.
                    I rest in peace. And I don't have to die to do it.
                    And I see things. Sometimes.
                    And I hear things. Sometimes.
                    And I wee myself. Often.
                    But who cares about that.

MARY   I do.

MOTHER   I could have a good life, actually.
                    If people listened. If people let me be where I need
                          to be.

In the past. Instead of trying to force me to live in
    their present. The present stinks.
The secret is to live in the past.
That's where I spend all the time I can.
It's the present I can't abide.
The past works. The past makes sense.
Or it's starting to. There's such a lot to think
    about.
The present's just chaos and makes no sense at all.
That's why I sleep a lot...

JOE   And our son –

KEVIN   Well I'm really like inarticulate and play computer
              games.

MARY   And our daughter –

MAZZ   I like fashion and magazines. And go out a lot.

JOE   And I teach Modern Studies.
              But you know that already.

              Pause.

              Funny sort of play.
              If I were management I'd be quaking in my boots.

MARY   Shoes.

JOE   What?

MARY   Shoes. Managers wear shoes.

JOE   Boots or shoes. Or barefoot too.
              I'd still be quaking.

MARY   And it's not quaking. It's shaking.

JOE   Shaking then. Whatever.
              Because if we put this into context.

MAZZ *and* KEVIN   Dad!!

JOE   Which we have to. Put it into context!
              Whether we teach Modern Studies or not.
              Because otherwise nothing makes any sense.

I mean look. Look at where we are.

I mean look. Look where we are.

In this Council Chamber.

With its fancy plasterwork and its wooden
    panelling.

It's all faded now but it's still beautiful.

And they built it this way

Because they valued democracy.

They felt democracy should have a grand and a
    special home.

And everyone wore their best clothes to attend.

The men wore dark suits and the women their
    smart hats.

The suffragettes spoke here:

Charlotte Despard and the Pankhursts.

The first coloured man to become a mayor was
    mayor here.

In 1913!

His name was John Archer. A good man. A brave
    man. We should remember him.

So many speeches spoken here.

Spoken by men and women who wanted to create
    a better world.

I'm proud we're here.

Proud this is the place in which our story is told.

And look.

A chair descends from the ceiling.

MARY   It's a lovely chair.

JOE   It's not Elsinore.

MARY   No. It's my lovely chair. That belongs in my
               lovely conservatory.

               Where I can sit and enjoy the sunshine.

               And where we can grow tomatoes.

               That really really taste of tomatoes!

               And I know you're going to say we can't really
                   afford it

               And it's funny, because I'm the one that's
                   supposed to be careful about money.

I'm the tax inspector.
But it's beauty.

JOE   It is. You are. Beauty.

MARY   It's worth more than any money.
And I know what you're going to say.
That it's not about us being special. Not about us
as individuals. It's not like Happy Families.
Or unhappy families. Not like Mrs Tax
Inspector. And Mr Tax Inspector.

JOE   And Miss and Master Tax Inspector.

MARY   And it's not about us being different from Mr and
Mrs Lawyer. And Mr and Mrs In The
Insurance Business or whatever.
It's not about individuals any more.
Can't be. It's about the whole thing.
Because everything's connected.
It's like you keep going on about there's no place
for the nation state any more. And that's the
flip side of globalisation.

JOE   You listened.

MARY   Of course I listen! I always listen to you.
Except when I don't.

JOE   And it's as if the machinery of our thoughts,
The stuff we have to use to think with,
Is as out of date and as marginalised
As this very theatre sometimes seems to be.
But we have to use it to understand.
Understand what we can about these times,
These unprecedented and unimaginably dangerous
times.
We have to try to find out. Hold up the mirror.
Make the brief abstract and chronicle of the time.
We have to try. Even if we fail.
We have to take the risk.
We have no other option.
That's me.
Kevin.

KEVIN   What?

JOE   It's you.

KEVIN   Me?

JOE   What did I just say?

KEVIN   Um.
         Well it's like this, see.
         I used to have this helicopter.
         It was amazing.
         I could fly all over the city!
         Weaving in and out the skyscrapers.
         Weeeeee!!
         And I had these fantastic machine guns that could
             flatten anyone who tried to get me.
         ACK ACK ACK ACK ACK!!
         And I was saving up for laser-guided bunker-
             busting bombs.
         But some pinheaded little fashion freak went and
             crashed the computer and I lost the game.
         And now I got to start all over again!
         I hate that!

MAZZ   It wasn't my fault! I was just watching an episode
             of *Sex and the City*!
         How was I supposed to know it had a virus!

JOE   Don't start! The pair of you! Just don't start!

KEVIN   Sorry, Dad.

MAZZ   Sorry. But if he'd just…
         Sorry.

JOE   It's your turn.

MAZZ   I think clothes really matter.

KEVIN   Fashion victim

MAZZ   Nerd.

MARY   Let her speak.

MAZZ   Clothes really matter because they tell you who
        you are.
        And if you wear nice things you're telling the
        world you're a nice person too. Whereas if
        you slob around in dirty jeans you're telling
        the world just that. That you're a slob. So I
        think a lot about it. And that night. I was
        getting ready for a party.
        And it was complicated.
        'Cause I wasn't really sure what kind of party it
        was.
        So I couldn't decide
        Skirt or trousers?
        And if it was skirt was it short or long?
        And if it was trousers was it trousers or jeans?
        And if it was trousers were they wide?
        Or were they tight? Only when I say wide
        I mean really wide.

MARY   Your trousers are dangerous.
        You keep falling over them.

MAZZ   But what about his? That look as if they're falling
        down all the time!

MARY   Yes, I know. Kevin's are ugly and silly...

KEVIN   Mum!

MARY   But yours are worse. Your tight ones are far
        worse.

MAZZ   But they've got to be like they were part of your
        skin!

MARY   Exactly. They should carry a health warning.
        These trousers can cause gangrene.

MAZZ   Trouser, Mum. They're called trouser.

MARY   Trousers or trouser. One day they'll cut off your
        circulation.
        Your feet'll turn black and drop off.
        And Dad'll have to carry you home in a
        wheelbarrow.

MAZZ   We talk about everything, me and Mum.
         Used to.
         Used to talk about everything.

MARY   That night
         I went to see my mum after work.
         I get off early on a Friday and I can pop in to see
                 her in the home.
         Which isn't a home at all.
         I mean the place she sits in.
         Hello Mum.

         The MOTHER *says nothing.*

         It's been a funny kind of week because someone
                 lost a whole lot of memory sticks.
         You know memory sticks, Mum, they use them in
                 computers to store information. Like compact
                 discs. Or floppy discs. Anyhow. Someone in a
                 different office went and lost a whole lot of
                 them.
         They got lost in the post.
         It's hard to believe.
         They had millions of people's details on them.
                 Anyway, even though it was nothing to do
                 with us they're still turning everywhere
                 upside down to look for them. Everyone's
                 desks and filing cabinets and everything.
         It's really funny.
         And Joe's fine. He's been marking exam papers to
                 earn extra money and he's been getting really
                 cross with the American firm that's running
                 the system and he's been on about the evils of
                 outsourcing.
         You know what he's like. Kevin's on his computer
                 as usual. And Mazz is fine and.
         Mum, I wish you'd say something.
         Mum, these days I have to force myself to come.
         Mum, are you angry at me?
         Anyway. Mazz has been talking about nothing
                 else but this party she's going to and.

MOTHER   I want to go home.

MARY   Oh. Yes, you say that. You always say that.
          You are at home, Mum.
          This is your home now.
          And it's nice here.
          It's nice and
          Sunny and there's a garden outside.
          And you got company and people to look after
                  you and make sure you haven't hurt
                  yourself.
          And
          Oh Mum, we can't manage you at home. We just
                  can't.
          And it's not so bad here.
          And oh God you've wet yourself.
          Nurse. Excuse me. Excuse me, nurse.
          And they promise to change her
          And I go away but I know
          I know it won't happen
          And the traffic's bad
          And Joe's marking his exam papers.

JOE   Bloody Americans!

MARY   And I cook tea.
          And everyone eats. More or less.
          And there's Mazz.

MAZZ   How do I look, Mum?

MARY   You look lovely.

MAZZ   You're not looking.

MARY   You look great.

MAZZ   You don't mean that.

MARY   No, I do. Honest.
          If I say you look great you think I don't mean it.
          And if I say I'm not sure you get upset.
          I can't do a thing right.
          But you do. Look great. Honest.

MAZZ   See, Mum, I like the top and the skirt and the
tights and the way everything clashes and
kind of goes together at the same time?

MARY   Enjoy yourself.

MAZZ   Thanks, Mum. Love you.

MARY   And she's gone.
And I tell myself not to worry.
And where's Kev?
Kev!
Why do I bother to ask?
And all of a sudden I'm so tired.
Turn on the telly, nothing on.
There should be more. There should be more to
life than this!
Should read a book. Can't find one.
Fall asleep.
I dream:
Our home is by the sea somehow,
Is it this house, ours anyway,
And there's a storm coming,
And I'm trying to organise,
I'm looking for wood to board up the windows,
And I can't find the nails,
And there's no one to help me,
And then suddenly the wave comes
Smash!
And everything's gone.
Not just broken up but kind of
Obliterated.
As if it was never there at all.
Aaaaaah!

JOE   Are you all right?

MARY   I had a bad dream.

JOE   Poor love.
You're tired.
Why don't you go to bed?
I've only got forty-three to go.

I'll be along in a minute.
No. No, I'll come now.
One of those moments.
One of those moments when you look back and
    you think:
I'm glad I did that.

MARY   And we go to sleep together side by side.
It's all you want, really.
People go on about good sex and orgasms
But I sometimes think that all you need
Is a warm loving body by your side.
Even if it does have bones and sharp angles.
And snores sometimes.

JOE   And I wake next morning and I've got a hard-on.
Oh
Haven't had one of those for ages
And
Oh... oh love...
Fast asleep.
And I'm stroking her
Ah... Stroking her where I know she likes it best
I don't understand how people can use the penis as
    a weapon
When a penis is such a tender thing
It just feels so tender and exposed
And vulnerable
All it wants is to be hiding somewhere safe and
    warm and
Ah
That's better
And she's

MARY   Having such a lovely dream

JOE   Up and down
In and out and up and down
So gently and so sweetly

MARY   And it's not, it's not a dream!

JOE   Oh my loved one

MARY	And it just breaks through! It just breaks through all the nonsense and the worry!
JOE	And where are we?
MARY	Oh we're somewhere so lovely
JOE	Where it's like time doesn't happen
MARY	Where it's like there's nothing but love
JOE	It's a garden where the flowers aren't fading
MARY	It's a pool where the water is warm.

JOE	It's as if you and me are speaking this amazing
	      language
	Where we don't need to say a single word and yet
	      we understand each other perfectly.

MARY	Somewhere we can never be alone.
JOE	Oh, my love, it's been so long I'm so sorry.
MARY	Don't be sorry, love, we all do what we can.
JOE	Yes.
MARY	Is Mazz back?
JOE	I'll go look. I'll make some tea.
MARY	And he goes And I'm sleepy and happy Or I would be But there's something at the back of my mind. Is she back?
JOE	Of course she's back.
MARY	She drinks too much.
JOE	They all do.
MARY	I worry.

JOE   Don't. She's fine. Here's your tea.
          We're out of milk. I'll get some more.

MARY   That feeling
          That feeling in my body
          Open. Happy.
          And outside the trees are in bud
          And I can hear
          The birds are singing.
          It'll be Easter soon.
          I must do the Easter tree.
          I must look out the eggs
          The lovely painted eggs I got from Prague.
          That I keep in an egg box somewhere
          And that Mazz thought were real eggs gone
                  mouldy
          And
          Suddenly the list pops up
          The long scrappy list in my head
          Of things to be done, and that don't get done,
          And that keep reproaching me.
          And it's become a job.
          A job on the list.
          I don't want it to be that.
          I want it to be a pleasure and a joy.
          And I want to hear the birds singing again.
          But they don't sound the same.
          I want the feeling back.
          I want that feeling back!
          But it's gone.

JOE   Don't see the sky much.
          There's always stuff to do.
          Things to worry about, but today,
          Look there it is the big beautiful blue
          And I feel on my face the gentle sunshine
          Oh God God how good to be alive.
          And then I make a terrible mistake.
          I buy a newspaper.

MARY   You shouldn't buy newspapers.

JOE   She says as I put the milk on the table.
And she's right.

Newspaper addiction. Very dangerous.
People like me should be forced into cold turkey
And allowed to read nothing but classic texts.
Catullus. Compulsory Catullus.
Catullus because he loved living.
Catullus because he loved loving.
Catullus. Catullus. Catullus!
Vivamus, mea Lesbia, atque amemus...
Oh my love let's live
So we can make love
Make love always and for ever.
Don't let's talk any more.
Don't let's talk of the sad old men
The sad dried-up old men
The prisoners of rules and regulations.
Let's love. Love while we can.
Soles occidere et redire possunt:
Nobis cum semel occidit breve lux
Nox est perpetua una dormienda.
For when the sun goes down
It can rise up again.
But when we go into the dark
We go there for ever.

MARY   You and your Latin.

JOE   Or the Gallic wars.
Nothing depressing about the Gallic wars.
I came I saw I conquered. End of story.
None of this anguish.
None of these endless outpourings from the
      despair industry.
You see they talk about a free press.
But if the press were really free would they let us
      read it?
I don't think so.
They let us read it because it depresses us.
Disempowers us.

Makes us believe there's nothing to be done.
And that suits them very well.

MARY   What are you thinking about?

JOE   There's been a great wave.
Swept in and smashed a river delta.
Swept hundreds of thousands of people away and
    smashed their houses.
Their shacks and their tin huts.

MARY   Don't start. We were feeling happy.

JOE   Drowned their livestock and destroyed their fields.
Swept away mothers. Fathers. Children. Old
    people and young.
Their corpses bloated and stinking among the
    debris.
Poisoning the water of those who survive.

MARY   We don't need to know this.

JOE   But it needn't have happened.
There were forecasts, but the government ignored
    them.
And the people didn't know because the
    government blocked news coming in from the
    outside world.
The country's run by generals.
Who deny their people help,
Because all they care about is power.
But what's the use of power
If you don't use it to make things better?

MARY   What's the use of reading papers which just make
    you all upset and don't make any difference?

JOE   We have to try to know. We have to try to
    understand.

MARY   Anyway you know what'll happen.
You'll be upset for a good few days
And you'll put money in a collecting tin if you see
    one

	And then it'll be something else. Zimbabwe again. Haiti or Afghanistan.
JOE	But if we can't feel for our fellow human beings what's the use of us?
MARY	We've got the house to clean. The ironing to do. Shopping. Exams to be marked.
JOE	And taxes to be collected. So we can buy more Trident missiles.
MARY	I'm not rising to that. I must do the ironing. I must get started on the ironing or we'll have nothing to wear. I must I must I must.
JOE	I'll do the shopping.
MARY	List's on the board.
JOE	And I've got the car keys. And I've got the plastic. Bye love.
MARY	Bye. Take care.
JOE	And that was the last time. The last time we spoke together.
KEVIN	And I'm in the city. And thanks to my pinhead sister I'm back at the bottom and I'm working my way up. I'd had to start again with nothing, I'd just been busted out of jail, And there was this car, and we took it. And he knew a guy in the red-light district And we went there. And this guy's a boss, not a big boss, Because I've only just started, but still a boss, And he's got this girlfriend needs picking up from the clinic.

So I goes out onto the street, and there's a car
    stopped at a red light,
And I take it.
You got to do that.
I mean, if you walk you're a nobody.
And you stay a nobody.
So I open the driver's-side door, and pull the
    driver out.
And he puts up a fight. So I hit him.
I don't have a gun yet.
But I'm strong, and soon he's on the ground, and
    he's bleeding,
So I jump in the car, and drive round to the clinic,
And there's this girl waiting. And she is so
    beautiful.
And she greets me with respect.
Because I'm not shy and spotty and self-
    conscious.
I'm black, and about seven feet tall, and I'm really
    toned,
And I would just so like to bang her up
But I daren't do that yet.
I'll do that later. Right now I'm only just
    beginning.

MARY   Kevin! Will you get off that computer!

KEVIN   In a minute, Mum...
    But why can't I stay?
    Why can't I stay here?
    Because everything makes sense here.
    It's mean and it's dangerous, but it makes sense.
    You do stuff, and stuff happens, but there's a kind
        of order to it,
    Because if you do good you rise up in the world
    And things get better.
    And it's not like here. It's not like here at all.

MARY   Kevin! Get off now!

KEVIN   And I go, because she's using that voice again,
        and when she uses that voice it gets right

inside my head and I lose the thread. And it's
no good any more.

MARY   I hate you spending all this time on the computer.

KEVIN   And I hate you always hassling me about it!
Why can't you leave me alone?
And that was the last thing. The last thing I said to
her.

JOE   And I'm not there.

MAZZ   And I'm sleeping in my bedroom
Because I went to the party
And everyone loved my outfit
And they had this amazing honey vodka
Only I had too much of it
And there was a fight and I was frightened on my
way home.

And now I'm dreaming.
I'm in this room and I'm fighting off sharks.
I'm all alone in this scary room and I'm looking
for Mum
Maybe I'm small again or something
'Cause I think she will help me
For some reason
But I can't find her anywhere.
I'm hitting them with a pepper pot
And I'm thinking This is ridiculous,
But it's all I can find.
And all of a sudden there's Kevin –
Kevin! – and he's helping me.
He's got this kick-arse enormous gun he's got
from his game
Only he's not firing it, for some reason
He's thwacking them over the head with it,
And I think Where's Dad?
Dad should be helping, but he's nowhere to be
seen
And all of a sudden Kev's attacking me
And I'm saying Stop it Kev!
Stop it I'm not a shark!

And then I looked at myself.
And I was.

And that morning I never saw Mum at all.

JOE   Shark steaks. They're selling shark steaks at the
            fish counter.
      And isn't that just so like them.
      They kill off the herring
      They kill off the cod
      And then they've got to start on something else
      Something else they can drive to extinction.
      And when they run out of animals
      It'll be us that they'll be selling.
      It'll be human steaks. Humanely harvested.
      From sustainable reserves to replant the rainforest.
      There'll be pre-packaged fingers
      For a lunchtime snack.
      Because every little helps.

KEVIN   I'm watching telly and Mum is doing the ironing.

MARY   I've got out the ironing board and I'm thinking of
            Mum.
      My mum. Grandma. Three clicks.
      That's how she had her ironing board when she
            did the ironing.
      And I hated her doing the ironing because it made
            me feel guilty.
      Like I couldn't be trusted to do it properly.
      But I know suddenly I'd give anything to have her
            ironing again.
      Have her out of that awful place where she sits
            and stares at emptiness
      And have her here being grumpy and judgemental
            again.

KEVIN   It was one of those Saturday-morning kids'
            programmes where they have a sexy female
            presenter and she ends up covered in pies and
            stuff and it's meant to be cool, I suppose, but
            it's really dull and I wish we had Sky, you can
            get better stuff on Sky, only Dad won't let us

have it because he thinks it's immoral or
something really really stupid.

MARY   I hate ironing.

JOE   I hate shopping.

MAZZ   I hate fighting.

KEVIN   I hate living...
Anyhow that's what I'm watching
I'd rather be back playing my game
my game in Sin City

MARY   And at last I'm doing the ironing

KEVIN   Mum's making those noises
Those noises she makes when she's ironing,
those kind of If I wasn't the only one who cared
    about these things round here then I wouldn't
    have to do this lousy ironing kind of noises
    that kind of go right through you and are so
    wrong because I do the washing up.

MARY   Phooey.

KEVIN   Well, sometimes.
So I'm not saying anything

MARY   And I'm not saying anything

KEVIN   And suddenly

MARY   I'm doing my blouse, one I really like, only it's
    got these ruffles down the front and it's a
    nightmare to iron
And I can't stand the noise the TV makes!
The music and the leery way they talk at you
And I'm just going to say
For heaven's sake put on the headphones
When
He comes.
It comes. This comes.
And it's like...
It's like...
A gargoyle

Something evil
Something very small but very strong
Here on my shoulder
Here on my right shoulder
And I know it means me harm.
I want to brush it off
I want to brush it off
But it won't go. It just won't go.
It just
Sticks there.
Hanging on
Laughing.
The evil thing that was
Draining my strength
This horrible
Evil
Thing.
And I can't bear it.
And then
And then it's gone.

JOE   There's a two-for-the-price-of-one on Anya
potatoes. Why are they always trying to sell
us Anya potatoes?
They're small and knobbly and you can't peel
them properly and they taste like soap. But
there they are. Every bloody week. Bloody
Anya potatoes. I want King Edwards.
Or Pink Fir Apples. Pentland Javelins.
Any bloody potatoes except the crap they sell.
And they're so proud of themselves for selling it
cheap.
But what's the point of it being cheap if it's crap!
And what's the point of it being cheap if it being
cheap means the poor bloody farmers can't
make a living from it?
Because then they might as well grow heroin
instead.
Or that stuff they use to make biofuel so we can
starve millions and wreck the environment all
at the same time.

That's brilliant, that is. That is capitalism in
    action.
And it matters.
If you can't get good potatoes it really matters.
No one believes me.
People laugh. But I tell them:
If people can't make a decent living growing
    decent food then we're done for.
We're going to starve ourselves to death.

MARY   And I
I'm on the ground.
I'm helpless on the ground.
I want to get up but I can't move.
I can't move my legs!
I can't move anything...
And I want to call out but no sound comes.
I'm wet.
Wet between the legs
I've pee'd myself
And he...
He shouldn't have to see this
A son shouldn't have to see that in his mother.

KEVIN   And they're just playing the number-one song
Which is total crap
When I hear this kind of cry
And look round
And it's Mum
It's Mum falling
It's like Mum's falling in slow motion
And then she hits the ground
Boof
And I don't know what to do.

MARY   And I'm
Lying on the floor
Crumpled somehow
I can see myself
Lying on the floor.
Crumpled.
And my son...

My son…
And I forget my son's name!

KEVIN   Mum. Mum!
What's happened? What's happened to you?
In the city no one, ever, helps each other.
And I never thought about it till now.
The way people are just left to bleed.
But I can't do that
And I can't do anything about what's happening to
          her.
In the end I call 999 like they do in the movies.

MARY   Ambulance.
He must have called an ambulance.
And they tie me to some stretcher thing and carry
          me downstairs.
And they are so grumpy
The ambulance men
So cross and grumpy because our stairs are steep
          and twisty and they have a lot of trouble
          carrying me downstairs, apparently, and
          they're so cross about it and I want to say
          Don't talk like that.
I can hear every word you say, you know
So just don't.
Don't talk like that
And the words are in my head
So clearly
So clearly in my head
But I
Can't say them.

JOE   Teabags. I hate bloody teabags.
They stuff them with sawdust and stain it brown.
But where can you get decent tea
You might as well drink water.
And the thing about this supermarket
Is that there's less and less food in it.
It's all school uniforms. Television sets.
Instant coffee. Precooked meals. And barbecues.
So people can get back to nature.

MAZZ   And I've gone back to sleep because I don't want
                to wake up
          My head's all fuzzy,
          And I have another dream, only I can't really talk
                about it,
          It's more a feeling
          A feeling of something nasty down there in the
                corner
          I'll sleep I'll go back to sleep and maybe it'll go
                away
          I'll sleep! I'll sleep!

KEVIN   In the ambulance
          I'm in the ambulance with my mum and I
          I don't know what to do
          I don't know what to say or anything
          Not that there seems to be any point in saying
                anything 'cause she's unconscious or
                something and never answers and I want to
                hold her hand
          But the seats are really awkward they're made so
                it's really difficult to hold the person's hand
                and anyway I haven't held my mum's hand
                for years and it's like I've forgotten how to.
          I want to be back
          I want to be back in the city
          Back inside my computer and I don't care if there
                are people out to get me
          Because it's safe in there.
          And if I was there I could do a job
          Or perform a task
          Or gain an extra skill
          Or something
          And then I'd be able to hold Mum's hand
          Or maybe I'd even be able to make her better
          But here…
          Nothing.
          Here I can do nothing.

MARY   I'm a parcel. I'm a parcel in a van.
          And I'm being carried somewhere I don't want to
                go

And it's so bumpy!
My head hurts
My head hurts
My
Head
Hurts.

KEVIN   And I want to ask
I want to ask what's happened
But I keep wanting to cry and I know I mustn't cry
And anyway I don't want to look stupid in front of
            the ambulance driver and she could almost be
            quite attractive
So I'm sitting there trying to look cool
Or something really stupid
And I can't be that good at it because she suddenly
            says
Don't worry about your mum she'll be all right
Or some shit like that
Because she won't be all right that's obvious
She can't be all right.
Not after this.

MARY   Young women.
Young women taking off my clothes and washing
            me
With their hard voices and their cold cold hands.
And no
May I?
Just taking off my clothes as if I belonged to them
And washing me.

JOE   And I've loaded all this crap into the car.
And I'm driving it home. Poisoning the air.
And whoever looks back on these times
On the last days of the so-called post-industrial
            age
Will ask themselves:
And how did they spend their time,
These last inhabitants of the lost world?
And how did they spend the last resources of their
            beautiful planet?

	On a two-for-one in the supermarket and driving it all home in the boot.
MARY	And then I see... this person. Here on this bed. She's been stripped. Stripped of her clothes. Stripped of her things. Stripped of her person. She has become a thing. A broken-down thing. Something to be thrown away.
KEVIN	And they've dumped me in the waiting room and I don't know what to do...
JOE	And I walk in the front door and say Hello! I'm home! But it seems like I'm the only one...
MAZZ	And I hear Dad and I wake up because I know something's wrong Dad! What's happened?
JOE	I don't know. Mum's gone. Kev's gone. Mum left the iron on
MARY	I don't recognise this person. Her face has fallen in. Her face is the wrong shape. Her face is a kind of catastrophe. There's something wrong with the cast of her eye. There's something wrong with the shape of her mouth. It's fallen down somehow. Who is this person? Who is she? And why am I alone? Why is there no one here? Mum! Is that you?
MOTHER	So there I was in the greengrocer's and I said Call that a potato? Call that a potato? That wretched withered little thing? I said That's a

tuber. You should be ashamed. Ashamed to
offer me such a wretched withered thing. And
call it a potato. What's happened to you, I
said, What's happened to you, Mr
Schickelgruber, you used to have such good
vegetables? And he said, Well the thing is,
Mrs Schmidt, since they stopped me going to
the market I just can't get the supplies. And I
said, I'm really sorry to hear that, Mr
Schickelgruber, I know you've got your
troubles but the thing is I need my potatoes.
And carrots and cabbage too and if you can't
give me any I'll just have to take my custom
elsewhere, and I marched straight out the door
and there on the pavement were a group of
young men in those awful uniforms everyone
seems to be wearing these days and they said
Can't you see the sign, are you blind?
And sure enough there was one of those stars
    painted on the door
And I wanted to say, But we're neighbours and
    we've known each other for years and I don't
    understand why he's turned into an enemy all
    of a sudden
But one of them said, Jew-lover
And another one
Spat at me
And I looked up, there were five of them and they
    were carrying clubs

And I
All of a sudden I was lost for words
So I went straight home and I did the ironing
And I should have been cooking lunch but I
    couldn't bear to somehow
So I did the ironing instead. I like ironing.
Lots of people don't believe me but I do.
No matter how bad you're feeling or how confusing
    things have become it's good to do the ironing.
It straightens things out somehow.
I started with the sheets and quilt covers

And the pillowslips and the tea towels and
    handkerchiefs
And then when I'd calmed down enough
I did my grandson's uniform.
And I shouldn't have done it in a way
It's his mother's job really
Only she's at work so much
Out at work when a son needs his mother
And it's a nice uniform
He looks so smart in it.

MARY   Mum, what are you saying?

MOTHER   I'm in the past, dear.
Like I said.
Now don't interrupt me.

MARY   But you were never there! I was never there!
And my son's not a Nazi!

MOTHER   Oh, I shouldn't be so sure of that dear.

MARY   But that's a terrible thing to say!

MOTHER   Is it dear? It seems so obvious to me.

MARY   Did you forget to take your pills?

MOTHER   What have pills got to do with it?

MARY   And I'm not German!

MOTHER   But that's where you're wrong dear.
That's where you're so terribly wrong.
We're all German now.
All of us. All German.

MARY   Mother? Mother where have you gone?
Don't leave me!
Mother! You can talk as much nonsense as you
    want but don't leave me alone!
I don't want to be alone!

A MAN *in the audience speaks up, an older man,
ordinary-looking in many ways, but very smartly
dressed.*

MAN   Excuse me. I wonder if I might be of any
                assistance.
        I hate to see someone in such distress.
        If you could just let me past? I am so sorry.
        And perhaps you could give me a hand to climb
                onto the stage?
        It is rather a climb. Thank you so much.

MARY   But who are you?

MAN   Excuse me. One moment.
        Silly of me. I always try to carry a business card.
        And I put it in a safe place and then I forget where
                it is.
        Men's clothes these days. So many pockets!
        Oh look. There they are. Here.

        MARY *reads the card and gasps*.

MARY   It must be a mistake!
        That can't be right!
        It can't be!

MAN   Oh I know. I'm so sorry. Such an ugly name.
        It can come as such a shock.
        Many many people feel just the same.
        Would you like a chair?

MARY   Thank you.

MAN   A glass of water?
        There.
        I'm sure you'll feel better in a moment.
        It is difficult, you see, to know how to break it.
        We could try a euphemism.
        English is especially rich in them these days.
        But Mr Passed Away? No.
        Mr Left Us To Go To A Better Place?
        Mr Gone To Sleep?
        Mr Termination? Dear me no.
        Though, come to think of it,
        Mr Euthanasia does have a certain ring.
        But then it's not quite accurate.

At the end of the day, there's no getting away from
   'Death'.
So I try at least to maintain a smart appearance.
To appear at least to look professional.
So there's no black cloak. No sinister hood.
No scythe. No sinister smile.
No grinning skull.
And a cadaverous appearance really does not help.
Oh, and I don't play chess.
Except in a certain gloomy Swedish film
Of a kind that never gets made any more.
I don't make many friends, unfortunately.
Pressure of business. You know how it is.
But perhaps at least we'll get acquainted.
My friends all call me Jim.

MARY   Am I dreaming?

MAN   Unfortunately not.
At least not in the sense you commonly
   understand it,
As being a transitory unreal experience
That will quickly pass and leave not a trace
   behind.
Something you go through and then return to
   normal.
I'm afraid that's not how it is.
That's not how it is at all.
Normal is something I seem to abolish and
   destroy.
And if you believe, as many do, and with good
   reason,
That life itself is just a dream,
Then I'm afraid that I'm the one to wake you.

MARY   I don't want this!
I don't! I really don't!

MAN   No of course you don't.
No one does.
It never ceases to amaze me,
This clinging on to life.

No matter how horrible or full of suffering life
    can be.
People will hold on, you see,
And I have to use so much effort to dislodge them.
And even so, even after years of the most dreadful
    torment,
So very few see me as I really am.

MARY   Who you really are? Who's that?

MAN   A friend.

MARY   You're not! You're not!

MAN   Now I won't say: Oh please don't cry.
Though I know that's the common response.
But under the circumstances it would be
    otiose.
Otiose: unnecessary. Superfluous. Rather a waste
    of time.
Because of course you need to cry.
I understand.
But allow me at least to offer you this.
A proper old-fashioned handkerchief.
I do hate tissues.
Of all the devices of the modern world,
I really do believe the tissue is the strongest
    evidence of a civilisation's decline.
And people say: but they save so much time.
Time for what I say. For living a joyful life?
But they never do.
It's only someone else that has to spend the time.
And far less agreeably. And for a pitiful wage.
Mopping up their garbage after them.
You see, you can't beat an old-fashioned
    handkerchief.
Cambric I think works best.
It doesn't irritate the delicate tissue of the nose.
And I like a little bit of colour.
It enlivens the drabness of the business suit.
Though I can always give you white if you'd
    prefer.

And don't think you need to return it.
I have an infinite supply.

As MARY *still cries, he magics a new
handkerchief into his breast pocket to replace the
one he has given her.*

MARY   It's just… It's just…

MAN   Please don't feel the need to hurry. You can take
your time.

MARY   I don't want to leave them! I love them so much!

MAN   Of course not. This is something that often gets
forgotten.
We tend to focus on the grief of those who are left
behind.
We forget the bereavement suffered by the ones
who die.

MARY   I know this sounds so silly, but I wanted to see my
Mazz get married.
Of course I wanted her to have a good job and
everything,
But I so wanted to see her walk down the aisle.
She'll make her own dress, you know, and it'll be
beautiful.
She's so talented.
And I wanted to see my Joe take her down the
aisle in a morning coat.
You know the things dads wear at weddings?
I know he'd hate to wear it, but he'd put it on for
her,
And he'd look so good in it.

MAN   I know he would. I know.

MARY   And I want to see Kev get a job making up those
awful games.
The ones he plays in his computer.
He's gifted too. He's got such an imagination.
And he understands how these things work.

MAN   He'll get to do that too.

MARY   And Joe. I so love Joe. He'll be so unhappy when
              I've gone.
         He's a good man. It's hard for him to be happy.
         And he loves the kids he teaches, I know he does,
         But I wanted him to be clear of that awful school.
         And all those terrible forms. All the stuff he has to
              fill in and hates so much.

MAN   Joe will be fine. You'll come to know. Though not
              in a way you currently understand. It's like
              your mother. Remember how she confused
              you? There are just so many different
              dimensions to time. You can be here. And
              somewhere else. And also really just here. All
              at once. Something to do with relativity. This
              way.
         Yes.
         It's time.

MARY   That body. That body over there.

MAN   Yes.

MARY   That's me.

MAN   I know.

MARY   That's horrible.

MAN   I know.

MARY   Did you do this?

MAN   It depends a bit upon your point of view.
         You could say it was me.
         If you happen to believe in the old-fashioned
              skeletal gent.
         The one with the scythe.
         The one they used to paint on old church walls.
         The one they used to use to frighten folk into
              confessing and seeing a priest.
         And into shelling out millions to pay for perpetual
              masses for their soul.

But now of course we're ever so much more
advanced.

MARY   What has happened?

MAN   We don't want to go into details.
I don't want to upset you by all that's happening
to the beautiful tissue of your brain.
When blood spills out, you see, it damages it.
Think of it like a typhoon.
Some parts of the river delta the wave devastates.
Others it leaves alone.
It's a mystery.

MARY   And did you do this?

MAN   I would prefer to say it was the blood vessel in the
crucial area of your brain.
The one that finally gave way under the strain.
The one that couldn't stand the pressure.
And perhaps it was the strain at work that gave
you the pressure.
Or the fatty food you so loved to eat.
Perhaps it was last week's chips.
There's no need to worry about those things.
It doesn't matter who or what did it.
What matters is it is.

MARY   I don't understand.
I don't want to go.
I can't bear to leave my children.

MAN   Now dear just you settle down
And I'll tell you a little story.
Stories always work best, I think,
For conveying important information.
There. That's better.
Are you sitting comfortably?
Then I'll begin.

So here I am one day
Just minding my own business.
When God comes up to me and says:
Death it just isn't good enough!

I'm sorry. It just isn't.
On second thoughts, says God,
No I'm not sorry.
I'm not sorry for anything.
After all, I'm God.
It's them who should be sorry.
Them humans.
Look at the mess they've made of the world.
Yes, I know I invented original sin but they were
    meant to ignore it!
Overcome it! Be stronger than it!
Instead, just look at it.
Look at the state of the world!
And what's far more serious is this:
They don't think of me at all!
All they think about are
Designer watches. Penis enlargers.
Debt management and bank accounts.
I've been intercepting their e-mail!
And as for their prayers...
Please God make me rich.
Please God make me famous.
Please God look after my dog.
Confirm her pedigree
And make her best in show!
But who's really the best?
Who's the one who's the source of every good?
Me! God!
And they're all forgetting me!
Death it just isn't good enough. Do something!
And I say:
With all respect Most Mighty Lord
And fountain of all knowledge
Haven't you forgotten quite how hard I work?
Already in the last one hundred years
Which as Your Eminence knows
Pass in but the twinkling of an eye
I've instigated two world wars
A magnificent programme of genocide
Much imitated, never surpassed –

Plus, and this, Lord, this is my masterstroke
An economic system that can kill
Two thirds of the world through war and
      starvation
And the other third through overeating and excess,
And also, Lord, in the process destroys the earth!
Not to mention, Your Magnificence, a little
      masterpiece like nuclear energy or the motor
      car
That kills them off in their millions!
And still you complain!
Why so dissatisfied, Magnificence, why so
      grumpy?
Haven't I done enough?
And God says:
Of course, friend Death, you've done superbly
      well
But can't you do a little more?
Look at Everyman.
And guess who he's pointing at?
Yes, you.
And what are you doing?

MARY   Can't remember.

MAN   You're doing the ironing.
And God says:
Can't you do something to make him remember
      me?
Friend Death, do what you can!
I want them to remember me!
And God was gone!
Poor fellow, ever since he disposed of God the
      Mother,
He's been completely gender-blind.
I watch Everyman a while.
I love watching humans do their ironing.
It's such a potent image of futility.
And I say: Good afternoon.
You jump.
I say

I have come to take you on a journey.
You don't look like a travel agent, says you, quite
     reasonably,
And anyway you book online.
But this is no holiday.
This is a journey from which you won't come
     back.
Your life is finished. It's time it came to an
     end...
But I'm not ready, you whine, as you all do,
Give me a little time.
But time is not allowed.
Do you want some money?
No I don't take money.
Not cash, not cheques, not credit cards.
Can I phone a friend?
But of course. Take someone with you if you wish.
It's horrible to go alone.
Perhaps my friends.
But no one will go with you.
Not your friends. Not your family.
Not the one that you most love.

MARY   How could I ask him?

MAN   How indeed.
         And so you're at a loss.
         And you remember your possessions.
         But they cannot help you.

MARY   And they tell us they're what matters!

MAN   Exactly. And so you know yourself to be cheated
             and deceived.
         And you think of everything good you have done
             in the world.

MARY   Precious little.

MAN   Exactly. Your good deeds are so feeble and weak
         And so they cannot help you.
         You try with all your might to understand
         And you call in all your five senses

To give you every scrap of information
About what was happening and how it was to be.
And they all swear to help you.
But they all have to leave you in the end.
Understanding, feeling, beauty, sight, smell,
        hearing, touch
All desert you.
You have to go to the place
The place where everyone goes,
And on the way you must confront your life.
All you've done
All you've left undone
All you were and all you could have been.
In the old story you could go to the church
And the church could absolve you.
But the church has dissipated all authority and
        power
And there is no one and nothing to help you.
And so you go
You go lonely into the darkness.

End of Act One.

ACT TWO

MARY   This place.
This dark empty place.
Where there are no shadows
This place where time stands still.
What is this place?

MAN   Think of it as a kind of house.
Desirable location, well appointed, good size.
Infinite up, infinite down.
No bathrooms of course.
No kitchen and no dining room.
But wonderful views.
An excellent location. None better...

MARY   You're not very funny.

MAN   I'm not joking, I assure you.

MARY   Do I stay here for ever?

MAN   Oh no. You move on. Everything moves on.

MARY   Moves on where?

MAN   On their way.

MARY   On their way where?

MAN   On their way to
The other place.

MARY   You're not being very helpful.

MAN   How could I be?
I can't tell you about
That place
Because you're not there yet.
And when you are there
I won't need to tell you.
Because then you'll know.

MARY   Know what?

MAN   The things you don't know now.

MARY   You are the most irritating man.

MAN   Thank you.

MARY   You're like a boss I used to have.
            He thought he knew everything.
            He thought he knew everything about the finer
                things in life.
            His secretary used to have to bring him special
                tea.
            And serve it in a special china teapot
            Because the stuff we drank wasn't good enough
                for him.
            And he knew fuck all. Pardon my language.
            Pompous fool. This was a while ago,
            And he looked a bit like the foreign secretary.
            So we used to call him Doctor Death.

MAN   What a coincidence.

MARY   That's very strange.

MAN   Fascinating. Memory traces. Flashing across your
                brain.
            Whose significance apparently
            Bears no relation
            To the value attached to them by the conscious
                mind.

            A chair appears.

MARY   My chair!

MAN   Of course. One thing at a time.
            No one wants to overwhelm you. Do sit down.
            And please don't be afraid.
            This is a natural process. Very natural.

MARY   Voice on a relaxation tape.
            The doctor gave it me to see if it would help my
                blood pressure.

Waste of time. Never relaxed me.
His voice just got up my nose.
This is a natural process. Very natural. Now you
      just let go.
Pompous fool. Made me tense up like anything.
Next thing you'll start sounding like an advert.

MAN   I probably will.
It's the subconscious mind you see.
Full of them. Often these days
A human's last conscious thought is of deodorant
      or toilet roll. You're relatively cultured.
You see this as a place where no shadows are
Because there is no sun to move around the sky
And no moon to softly glow at night.
It's all part of the western tradition. It's Hades, or
      the underworld.
It probably comes from your husband.
      Fascinating.
Now if you'd been brought up in the east
You'd be in Naraka, and everything would seem
      very different.
You'd be in a dark, frozen plain surrounded by icy
      mountains
And continually swept by blizzards.
You would live there naked and alone, while the
      cold raises blisters upon your body.
And you would live there for the time it would
      take to empty a barrel of sesame seed.
Assuming that is one only took out a single seed
      every hundred years.
Assuming, of course, you had a bad conscience.
It all comes when you review your life.
When you see it unscrolling before your eyes.
I'll be curious to meet your husband, when his
      time comes.
I wonder if he'll see Cerberus, the three-headed
      dog
Or dreaded Pluto with his lovely Persephone.
As for you, how will your judgement come
Will you see Jesus sitting on his throne?

MARY   There's Mazz and Kev and Joe.

MAN   Ah. That's how.

MARY   Poor loves.

MAN   Look at them waiting.
Hoping against hope
You can return.

MARY   I hope Kev's remembered to have a shower.
I hate it when I have to tell him.
He gets so hurt…
And I hope Joe's remembered to change his shirt.
I'm so proud of him.
He cares so much. He works so hard.
I always want him to look his very best.
Mazz always does. It amazes me,
We should have produced someone quite so
       glamorous.
Oh my loves
I wish I could reach out to you
And take you by the hand and say
It's all right
Don't be afraid
I'm still here
I love you
I always did
I always will

MAZZ   Me and Mum used to watch *Casualty* a lot.
And sometimes I'd dream of being a nurse, and a
       bit battered and troubled but really caring.
And even though terrible things kept on
       happening, a mum might be dying of cancer
       while her baby son was suffering from heart
       disease, or something,
And things often looked really bad, somehow
You knew things would get better by the end.
They'd all be clustered round a trolley
Sticking needles into them
And shouting technical things
And making them better.

But it's not like that here.
No one seems to be doing anything.
Or to know about anything.
And all we do is sit about and see if she wakes up.
And all the patients on the telly look ill but
    basically okay
In their hospital gowns.
But the thing they've put Mum in is just awful.
She doesn't look like a person at all.
I can't bear it.
And Dad's just sitting there looking really
    traumatised.

JOE   I've forgotten what a gerund is.
It's different from a gerundive.
But I can't remember what the difference is.
And in Latin, that really matters.
I saw a film once about a man being brainwashed
    by the Chinese.
Or maybe the North Koreans.
Whoever the villains were at the time.
He was in solitary confinement
Like in Guantanamo
And to keep himself sane
He imagined the house extension he'd build when
    he got home.
He'd imagine it being built up
Brick by brick
As if his imagination was projecting it onto the
    blank cell wall.
Latin's like that.
It's like a building in the mind.
You build it bit by bit, word by word,
Block by block.
And it's like it strengthens the inner mind.
And people say, what's the use of it,
It's got nothing to do with the real world...
But that's the whole point of it.
That it's not real life.
It's a different place.
A place inside.

An ordered place.
Somewhere life makes sense. We all need that.
Kev understands.
Especially now, in this terrible place we're all in.
But it's gone.
The gerund and the gerundive.
Gone.
Latin has gone.

KEVIN   I've been looking up strokes on the web.
Apparently they're the most common cause of
          death in the whole world.
More common than shootings or bombs or traffic
          accidents.
More common than AIDS or starvation or any of
          the really big diseases.
More common than cancer!
But we never read about strokes.
They're never in the TV news.
And we never hear about them at all.
That is so weird.
And I want to ask if what Mum has got
Is ischaemic or haemorrhagic.
Apparently it matters.
Ischaemic is what happens when a little bit of shit,
          a blood clot or something,
Blocks an artery and blood can't get to the brain.
And you can do something about that.
If you can get at it on time.
You can give a clot-busting drug or something that
          restores the blood supply.
But they're not giving that to Mum.
So it must be the other one.

Pause.

And the other one means a blood vessel burst
And there's bleeding in the brain
So it gets really damaged.
Some kind of flood. Or like the busting of a dam.
Wipes out everything in its path.

MAZZ Me and Mum saw a film once about a man who
    had a stroke.
  And like Mum, he was unconscious.
  But the doctors, the nurses, they all cared.
  And they believed that they could do something.
  And when he came round
  He couldn't speak.
  There were speech therapists.
  There were two speech therapists!
  Who were there to help him talk again.
  And they were both so beautiful and dedicated and
    French.
  One of them could tell he understood what they
    were saying
  And discovered he could blink, once for yes, twice
    for no,
  And she worked through the alphabet with him,
  Letter by letter,
  And when he blinked yes she wrote the letter
    down.
  And she went on doing that until they'd written a
    whole book.
  A book about what it was like to be him.
  And it was so lovely and everyone cried.
  And I'd do that for Mum.
  If I knew how or there seemed any point to it.
  But no one's come.
  No one.
  We've just been left here in this horrid little room
  And everyone's given up on Mum
  And I just can't bear it!
  It's like
  It's like we've ended up in a place where stories
    just don't happen
  Except the sad ones.
  It's a place where nothing makes any difference
  Nothing makes any sense.

KEVIN I wish this was a game.
  A game where you'd shrink yourself down, it'd be
    like that movie

You'd get yourself miniaturised
So you could travel through the bloodstream,
Like in a special submarine,
And you'd meet all these dangers,
Like white blood cells or viruses
And you'd have to find your way up to the brain
So you could discover what kind of stroke it was.
And you'd have won yourself special powers on
    the way
So that once you got there
You could clear it up
And winning the game would mean
Mum was better and could come home again.

JOE   Mary just makes this rattly kind of bubbling
          sound.
      It's just fluid, that's what they say
      It's trapped at the back of her throat, apparently,
          and the air she breathes passes through it
      And that's where the noise comes from.
      It doesn't mean that she's in pain.
      It could go on for days.
      They say.
      I try to tell myself that soon it's going to stop.
      And I try to believe it,
      But I can't. I just can't.

MAN   An old woman in a mental home. Heart failure.
      A young woman in the Middle East. Burnt to
          death.
      Self-immolation.
      Apparently she loathed her husband.
      A young man in the south.
      Slowly being clubbed. Twitching.
      Seems to belong to the wrong ethnic group.
      Older man in the west.
      Eating himself to death.
      It all takes a very long time.
      He's complaining life's just meaningless
      And besides, he says, the service is just so slow.
      Baby in a transit camp. Malnutrition. Diarrhoea.

Woman in a prison cell.
Slowly dying of solitude.
Woman in hospital bed. Brain tumour.
There's a cancer of the lung.
Cancer of the kidneys.
Of the throat.
Cancer of the penis.
There's one being drowned. Thrashing about.
Radioactive poisoning.
Alcohol. Alcohol. Alcohol.
There's an overdose.
A child dying from lack of love.
Another of leukaemia.
Road-traffic accident.
Throttled by a noose.
Smothered by a pillow.
Raped and left to bleed to death.
Died in her sleep.
Quiet and peaceful. A rarity.
Gunshot wounds.
Fell down a mountain.
Choked on a piece of fruit.
Heroin. Massive heart attack.
And amid all these gasping sobbing blaspheming
    screaming sounds
Sometimes I think I hear a greater lamentation:
The slow majestic dying of the planet Earth.

MARY   I was born so helpless!
I could not even lift my head!
That's why I had to trust
Those who cared for me.
And I know they loved me but
When they told me I was bad
Or was not worthy to be loved
That's what stuck somehow
And later, look, when they took me each morning
    to that place
Where I was not happy,
That school they said was good for me
And it was my fault if I was miserable there.

Almost everything they taught me was false.
All the information that they gave me
Everything I knew about myself and the world.
I can see them, I can see them lying
I can see the falsehoods spill out of their miserable
    mouths.
I don't think they meant to lie to me
I think they did their best
And in their way
They loved me.
It was very hard to distinguish false from true.
My children helped
Even when they hated and rebelled against me
Because especially then
They held up the mirror
Whose reflection I needed to see.
I loved a man
And lived with him.
It was very hard,
I think
But he loved me as best he could
And we tried hard
To bring up our children
And know they are loved in the world.
I made many mistakes, I think.
I did what I could.
My life seemed so big
When I was living it
Now it seems so small.
How weak we are, we humans.
How frail our light.
How easy for you to put it out.
I spent a lifetime becoming myself
Giving birth and bringing up my children
Loving my husband as best I can
I always wanted to create a better world.
How feeble it all seems. Pathetic really.
Because you can sweep it away
So simply, without even the blink of an eye.
And it means nothing, my death,

My husband's sorrow, my children's loss
Count for nothing in the greater sorrow of the world.

MAN   Finally for now
           Death by a touch, a caress.
           A stroke.

KEVIN   Nothing much seemed to happen

MAZZ   It wasn't like a death in the movies

KEVIN   One minute there we were beside her
           Listening to that terrible noise

MAZZ   Trying to believe it wasn't hurting her

KEVIN   And then it stopped.

           Pause.

MAZZ   And we sit there kind of stunned.
           And I hug Dad.
           And Dad

JOE   I can't believe. I can't believe it's happened.

KEVIN   And the nurses make sympathetic noises.
           And I think Dad has to fill in a form.

MAZZ   Mum, we'll go home and fetch your favourite dress
           And Mum. I promise I'll design a hospital gown.
           A better gown for people to wear in bed.
           I'll find out what the nurses need and everything.
           And I'll make it. And you'll be proud of me.
           Bye, Mum. Goodbye.

KEVIN   Bye, Mum. I'll make that game. I promise.
           So people understand things like strokes better.
           And then you'll know I've not been wasting my
               time.

JOE   Goodbye my love.
           I can't say anything.
           Goodbye. Goodbye.

MAN   Time for the dance, I think.
           Something slow, I think, to begin with.

> Slow and a little solemn.
> Perhaps a pavane.
> Will you join me?

MARY   But you can't dance now!
           No one can dance now!

MAN   On the contrary my dear.
           And may I say you look charming in that dress?
           People dance most at moments of greatest stress
           In 1518, in the city of Strasbourg,
           Five hundred people danced in the streets for
                weeks on end
           And all in response to the plague.
           This is the dance they painted on church walls
           You see me as a skeleton there
           And smiling a bony grin
           And I invite everyone to join me in the dance.
           Pope, Emperor, Empress, knight,
           The common woman and man
           All come and join me, willingly or not
           Some are sullen, some frightened,
           Some indifferent. Some laugh. Most weep.
           But they all have to join me just the same.
           It's only natural. For as long as humans have
                walked the earth
           You have formed the circle
           And trod the measure of the dance.
           The dance of the seasons. The dance of the tides.
           The dance of every cell in the human body.
           The dance to death
           And the dance to life again.
           Dance humans dance!
           Dance away your wretched lives!
           Lay down your burdens and dance!
           Aren't you glad to hear it's all over!
           Fret no more in your useless sorrow
           Grieve no more in your pathetic grief
           Dance humans dance your way to darkness!

Ideally, the stage is full of as many DANCERS *as the theatre can manage. This should be a moment*

of the most vivid noise and colour and movement.
MARY, caught up with the rest, is whirled
towards KEVIN, then MAZZ, then finally, JOE.

KEVIN   Don't go, Mum. I miss you! Don't go!

MAZZ   Love you, Mum. Love you!

By the time she reaches JOE everyone else has
gone.

JOE   Oh love, how good to see you here again!
           Why have we been apart so long!
           It's like there's been some terrible
                   misunderstanding
           But it's over now and at last we're all together
                   again.
           I don't understand what's kept you.
           Why can't you speak?
           Why can't you speak to me?
           I know why.
           I'd forgotten for a moment but I know why.
           You're dead. You shouldn't be here.
           You're dead! You're dead!

And she's gone.

           A dream.
           Terrible dream I had.
           And I wake up
           And I'm alone.
           Beside me is a hollow like a grave.
           It'll always be inside me this blank space. This
                   grave.
           No one to make a cup of tea for in the morning.
           No one to bring me a cup of tea.
           No one to hold in the cold dark night
           No one to trust. Solitude.
           What will I do when I reach out to you and you're
                   not there
           What will I do when I come home and the house is
                   empty.
           What will I do?
           What will I do?

He goes.

MARY   Joe? Joe where are you, where've you gone?
          There's no one.
          I must have become a ghost.
          What do you do when you're a ghost?
          Do you walk down the corridors alone?
          There's Mum. Mum! Mum!
          I'm frightened.

MOTHER   Can't stop. Must rush.

MARY   Where are you going?

MOTHER   I've got to catch a train.
          The Germans said they'd shoot anyone who was
                left behind.

MARY   Mum –

MOTHER   They did say we could take a suitcase.
          The Germans aren't so bad.
          And they told us exactly how big it can be.

MARY   Mum –

MOTHER   Trouble is, it's so very small.
          Look at it. Look how small it is!
          And you've got to pack your whole life in there.
          And what do you put in?
          And what do you leave out?
          Should I put in warm underwear?
          They say it's rest camps.
          Rest camps in the east.
          They didn't say if it would be hot or cold.

MARY   Mum, you're having that bad dream again.

MOTHER   It was a gentleman told me.
          Ever such a nice gentleman.
          Wonderfully polite.
          And anyway we're all in the same dream.
          All of us. In the same bad dream.
          It started when your father came back from the
                war.

MARY   But I wasn't born then!

MOTHER   You were the best bit dear. The best bit of the
                   dream.
            Though when you came you made me suffer.

MARY   I didn't mean to!

MOTHER   When your father saw me he was horrified.
            I had tubes coming out of everywhere.
            I was all tubes. Never again!
            He said I'm never putting you through that again!
            And we slept in separate beds after that.
            He took out the double while I was in hospital.
            And when I came home with you
            There were two singles.
            And that's how it stayed.
            Mind you, I think it was just an excuse.
            He never quite had the appetite for it when he
                   came back from the war.
            He just did it for me because he knew I wanted a
                   baby.
            And then he stopped.
            And that was that.
            There was no arguing with him.
            There never was.
            He wasn't a bad man, your father.
            You know he wasn't a bad man.
            It was just. Something happened to him.
            Something happened to him in the war.
            Something he saw.
            And he was so young when they sent him away.
            He was just a boy.
            He'd always say: Those were the best years of my
                   life,
            When I was away.
            And then he'd say:
            Of course you just remember the good times.
            And then he wouldn't say a word.
            He was on the buses. Same as me.
            He was on the buses before the war
            And he was back on the buses when he got back.

On the same route. The 355. There and back
    again.
He liked that.
He liked things to stay the same.
So when they brought in one-man operation
He couldn't stand it and he left.
He took the redundancy money
And we went on one holiday to the south of Spain
And he bought a satellite dish.
And instead of sitting at the wheel driving his bus
He sat at home and watched the telly.
He'd watch the History Channel. All day.
They were showing a history of the Second World
    War.
And one day I was bringing him his cup of tea
And he was crying.
There were dead bodies all over the screen.
So thin they looked like skeletons.
And some of them were alive.
Terrible. Terrible.
And the dead ones were being bulldozed into a pit.
Hundreds of them. Hundreds.
And he kept saying
I was there. I was there. I saw it
I saw it!
And the next day he took his stroke and died.
That's when I understood.
That's when I understood
What he'd been bottling up all those years.
Poor man.
You want to keep it bottled up.
You want to pretend it all happened somewhere
    else
And had nothing to do with you.
It was other people who did it.
Them people, the evil ones,
And had nothing to do with you.
But you can't keep it in.
You can't keep it boxed up.
We all suffer.

We're all Germans
And we're all Jews
And he knew that.
And that's why he went there
And I'm going to rescue him.
So I've to go on the train
I've to go to that place because that's where I'll
    find him.
And I'll bring him back.
He doesn't belong there.
None of us do.
I'll find him there and I'll bring him back home.
And don't you try to stop me.
I'll manage.
And don't you tell me to sit down and not go
    home.
Because that's where I'm going.
Once I've found him.
We're going together.
We're going home.

MARY   You did this.

MAN   She did it herself.
Memory, you see.
You create the world from memory.
You'll see. You'll understand.
You're next.

We start to see a CHILD *on a swing.*

Remember her?
Farewell.

MARY   That's me.
That's me!
In the backyard.
I'd done something terrible.
I'd set fire to the house.
Just the waste-paper basket but it felt like the
    world.
I'd been playing with matches to see what they did.
Because they'd told me not to.

And I was so frightened
And Mum wouldn't comfort me.
She said I was a bad girl
And I should be punished.
And I ran away and I sat on the swing.
And I swung back and forth and I said

And the CHILD *joins in with her.*

I am
Mary Jane
Spring
And I live
In 55 Shore Street
Anstruther
Fife
Scotland
Great Britain
Europe
The World
The Solar System
The Universe.

And the CHILD *stops swinging.*

And here we are.
It's over now.
It's over now and everything's better.
Everything's all right again.
Shall we go home?
We can go now.
Over there where the light is.
That's home.
Shall we go?
Shall we go home?

The CHILD *nods. They go home.*

JOE   It's a year. A year goes by. Fifty-two weeks. I
        think.
        Fifty-two bottles. Fifty-two bottles of gin. Used to
        drink malt. We used to drink malt together.
        Loved it. So I couldn't.

And you. Me. You go through the motions. You do
what you've always done. You go to work.
Mark exam papers. You say Fine thank you.
Because they may say How are you but they
don't really want to know. No one really
wants to know. They really just want to leave
you alone. And so there you are. Alone. And.
What can you do. What can you do. You go
through the motions. And time heals. Time
heals, they say, but that's just crap! That's just
total crap! Time doesn't heal anything. Time
just makes things worse! All time does is
make you push it down, push it way down
below the surface so everything looks normal
and no one has to bother with it any more.
And –

Pause. Tears in his eyes.

MAZZ   This is so difficult!
You have to imagine
Someone say lying helpless in a bed
Or someone changing for an examination
Needing
Something that's easy to take on or off
But doesn't leave you feeling naked and stupid
and vulnerable.
So it's got to tie up easily.
Velcro's obvious.
But it's also got to be flat
So if you lie on it a long time
It's not going to get uncomfortable.
And the material's got to be nice to wear
And not crease uncomfortably
And be hard-wearing
Because it'll be worn hundreds and hundreds of
times
And it has to be easily washed
And easy to dry
And ideally not need pressing
And it's got to be made cheaply

And I want it to look good as well!
I don't know if I can do this, Mum.
And all my friends in college laugh at me.
Because they're designing
Amazing frocks and hats and shoes.
I was modelling a dress for a friend of mine
And it was a bugger to wear.
I said to him:
Look I can hardly breathe
And I can hardly move my arms
And I can't walk in it
And how am I supposed to go to the loo?
And he said:
But darling you look fabulous.
And the thing I don't get about you,
Darling,
He said
Is why you persist in designing
Hospital gowns for fat old ladies
Who are so sick and gaga they'll never know the
        difference?
And I said:
At least they'll be able to go for a pee.
And anyway
Just because.
And I will finish it, Mum.
I'll finish it for me.
I'll finish it for you.

KEVIN   I'm in a body. Maybe Mum's.
Maybe yours. Maybe mine.
Maybe anyone's.
And I'm in a little boat
Travelling through the bloodstream
To inspect the damage and repair it.
I've left the city far behind.
Can't imagine why I spent so much time
On that useless horrible game.
This one's so difficult
But it's so amazing.
I'm working to imagine it

And learn the machine language
So I can really make it happen.
And the boat goes on
Through all the major organs.
Up through the neck
Behind the mouth, the nose, the eyes,
And then we're travelling through
The spongy matter of the brain
With its amazing labyrinths and spirals.
And there's other boats up there with us,
And that's really hard,
Inventing the ways we can cooperate,
And we're slowly, carefully,
Repairing the damage
So the body will be safe
And the world made whole again.
And I don't know if I can do it, Mum.
But I'll try. I'll try. I'll try!

JOE   So this is me.
Sitting in her chair.
In her old conservatory.
Sitting in the space we don't need any more.
That we don't need because she's gone.
Because the children have gone.
And because suddenly the house feels big and
        empty.
They had to go. The children.
They had to. Had to go.
And I'm left behind.
Sitting in her chair.
Looking at the plants she loved and looked after.
And that I've neglected.
And there's a heap of exam papers on the kitchen
        floor.
Waiting to be marked.
It's that time of year again.
But I can't do it.
I've just understood
I can't judge any more.
Everyone does their best, I'm thinking,

And I've no right to put a number on it.
I don't even think I can teach any more.
I've nothing left to say.
In my last class I told them:
We're living through the end, I said,
The end of an era,
The end of a historical time.
It's time for a new beginning.
And you're the ones, I told them,
You're the ones to make it happen.
And then I walked out the classroom and I came
     home.
And I sat down in the chair.
And all I want to do just now
Is watch the daylight slowly fading
And maybe start to think about the day
I will get up and cultivate this place again.

Pause.

And I do get up.
I do get up, a bit to my surprise.
I do get up but it hurts.
It's as if grief has injected
Some kind of poison into all my limbs
So they ache and it hurts to move.
But I stand up, I stand up anyway
And I move on, limping slightly.
And I tell myself
It's not just the end.
It's not.
It's not.

End.

A Nick Hern Book

Every One first published in Great Britain in 2010 by Nick Hern Books Limited,
The Glasshouse, 49a Goldhawk Road, London W12 8QP

This revised edition published 2016

Every One copyright © 2010, 2016 Jo Clifford

Cover photography: Richard Davenport; cover design: Guy J Sanders

Designed and typeset by Nick Hern Books, London
Printed in Great Britain by Mimeo Ltd, Huntingdon, Cambridgeshire
PE29 6XX

A CIP catalogue record for this book is available from the British Library

ISBN 978 1 84842 574 3

Other Titles from Nick Hern Books

TO
10
OF EVERYTHING

TOP 10 people to thank for helping me to write *TOP 10 of Everything*

1. My best friend
Jesus Christ: for His utter belief in me.

2. My beautiful wife
Jenny: for her brilliance in the Spirit.

3. My inspirers
Brian Houston, Steve Penny, Danny Guglielmucci, Dave Cartledge, Wayne Alcorn, Paul Scanlon and C.H. Spurgeon!

4. My armour bearers
Gerard Keehan, Glyn Barrett and Colin Davies.

5. My assistants
Hazel Hague and Chris Denham.

6. My Dad
Dr Alan Gilpin: for the inspiration of writing 20 books.

7. My Mum
Sheila Gilpin: for the gift of determination.

8. My Pastors
Peter Aspin, Chris Peterson and Colin White: for their spirit in the formative years.

9. My Church
Hope City Church: for being daring enough to be a Goliath-slaying church.

10. My son
Ryan: for his enthusiasm for life.

OF EVERYTHING

500 nuggets of
wisdom and advice
to help you excel
in Christian leadership

Dave Gilpin

MONARCH
BOOKS

Mill Hill, London and Grand Rapids, Michigan

First published in the UK in 2003 by Monarch Books,
Concorde House, Grenville Place, Mill Hill, London NW7 3SA.

Illustrations by Bridget Gillespie

Distributed by:
UK: STL, PO Box 300, Kingstown Broadway,
Carlisle, Cumbria CA3 0QS;
USA: Kregel Publications, PO Box 2607,
Grand Rapids, Michigan 49501.

ISBN 1 85424 634 8 (UK)
ISBN 0 8254 6232 0 (USA)

British Library Cataloguing Data
A catalogue record for this book is available
from the British Library.

Printed and bound in Great Britain by Bookmarque Ltd

Book design and production for the publishers by
Gazelle Creative Productions Ltd,
Concorde House, Grenville Place, Mill Hill, London NW7 3SA.

Introduction

Behind everything you see is something you don't see. This book is designed to outline nuggets of wisdom that often remain invisible behind thriving churches and ministries. Mixed with a touch of humour, *Top 10 of Everything* looks into the Private World, the Practical World, the Handy Hints World and the Wide World of Knowledge. It gives advice on many subjects that may prove to be invaluable to established and up-and-coming leaders. Read it all at once or read it one Top 10 at a time. This book can also provide new preachers with an opportunity to "borrow" some of the Top 10 outlines to create lively and dynamic sermons.

Enjoy and be inspired!

Dave Gilpin

Foreword

Top Ten of Everything manages to be both thoroughly entertaining, and amazingly comprehensive on the subject of leadership at the same time. In fact, for somebody who is currently writing a book on leadership, it is *annoyingly* comprehensive and one of those rare things – a book for people who don't actually like reading books.

This is a book to keep in the car, at the office, or anywhere else where you might have a few minutes' reflection and need to dip into something that will challenge, inspire and amuse you. Take my advice and read one of these pages each day, meditating on it throughout the day (although you won't be able to resist looking at the days ahead). Used like this, it'll give you 50 days of spiritual nourishment – vitamin therapy for the soul – which will do you good. If you doubt me try one of my favourite sections, "Top Ten ways to avoid being yesterday's leader". There is so much concentrated wisdom here. Brilliant! (The minute I read extracts to my staff, they wanted copies, and promptly made bootleg copies of the whole thing.)

So, don't just stand there – start reading today.

Rev. Eric Delve
Area Dean of Maidstone

in the

Private World of
a Christian Leader

•

Practical World of
a Christian Leader

•

Handy Hints World of
a Christian Leader

•

Wide World of Knowledge of
a Christian Leader

Contents

TOP 10 of Everything in the Practical World of a Christian Leader

TOP 10 of Everything in the Handy Hints World of a Christian Leader 71

TOP 10 of Everything in the Wide World of Knowledge of a Christian Leader 97

in the

Private World of
a Christian Leader

Sometimes, you don't need to pray more, but play more.

Re: fresh as a daisy

The freshness factor can make the difference between a leader just going through the motions and a leader excelling in ministry. It definitely makes the difference between enjoying the journey and just enduring it! A routine in life, as well as a routine in a Sunday service, is fine when it's fresh. A hymn sandwich should never be rejected on the basis of predictability but on the basis of degree of freshness.

How fresh are you?

Here are the top 10 ways a leader can keep fresh.

TOP 10 ways a leader can keep fresh

1. **Be true to your God-given personality**
   Stop copying someone else's life. Stop copying someone else's ministry. Be free to be you and be faithful to what makes you tick.

2. **Be aware of what God is endorsing**
   Stop trying to force open closed doors. Look to see where the hand of the Lord is and be engaged in what He is engaged in.

3. **Be open to reinvention**
   It's important to reinvent the wheel regularly. Changing the way you do things, the way you think about things and the way you look can put the zing back into life. (This is your excuse to go shopping.)

4. **Be a super-visor**
   Don't just have a vision for one thing. Have a vision for ministry, a vision for home and a vision for health. Super-vision looks at the whole, not just the part.

5. **Be released from failure**
   Don't stay in the place of failure. Get up, pick up your mat and walk into your God-given future. Failure is a learning curve to success.

6. **Be humorous**
   Have a sense of humour. Have a good laugh at the funny side of life. Seriousness can be a health hazard.

7. **Be committed to the cause**
   Don't sweat over all the small stuff. Keep the main thing the main thing.

8. **Be intimate with God**
   There is a place of refreshing in the presence of God. Ask Him to take your burdens and give rest to your soul.

9. **Be fit**
   Sometimes you don't need to pray more, but play more.

10. **Be around people that invigorate**
    Some people take from you and don't give back. Others give to you and expect something back. Others are simply glad you're around. Find your Lazarus, Martha and Mary and visit regularly.

Top 10 ☆ Bible Extra ☆ Matthew 11:28–30,
Acts 3:19, Romans 15:32, 2 Timothy 1:16

Yesterday's hero

You are God's chosen vessel. God's work on earth is either limited by the vessel or accelerated by the vessel. He has no plan B and rarely will God work outside of His partnership with His people. Being committed to the "increasing measure" is the key to being today's leader and not becoming yesterday's leader. They say that a rut is just a coffin with the ends knocked out. To be today's leader is to come out of the rut and be enlarged and expanded by the hand of the Lord.

Here are the top 10 ways to be today's leader and not yesterday's leader.

TOP 10 ways to avoid being yesterday's leader

1. Increase the capacity of the vessel

You are God's vessel. He will expand you, stretch you, tear you and make you. The greater the character and the greater the skill, the greater the opportunity for God to use you.

2. Increase the cleanliness of the vessel

You are God's vessel. Contamination is as bad as containment. Be a forgiver, keep pure motives and don't be distracted.

3. Increase the clarity of the vessel

You are God's vessel. Stay focused on the cause on which God has sent you forth.

4. Increase the confidence of the vessel

You are God's vessel. Don't just hide in the corner. Come out and be filled with the Spirit and sent to the masses. You were born for such a time as this.

5. Increase the content of the vessel

You are God's vessel. Wisdom is collected by meditating on God's word and listening to His voice. Be filled with His wisdom and His ways.

6. Increase the credentials of the vessel

You are God's vessel. What are you known to be? Timothy entrusted what he had learnt to "faithful men"! What reputation are you developing right now?

7. Increase the consistency of the vessel

You are God's vessel. Be strong in every area of your life. Be strong when the headwinds blow. Be strong when you feel like giving up. Be strong!

8. Increase the contact of the vessel

You are God's vessel. Salt isn't effective unless it's out of the salt shaker. Stir up the gift of God within you and exercise your gift upon the people you're called to.

9. Increase the cry of the vessel

You are God's vessel. According to your desire, be it unto you. Knock and the door shall be opened. Seek and you shall find.

10. Increase the consideration of the vessel

You are God's vessel. Three things remain but the greatest is love. Let love be your motivating force.

Top 10 ☆ **Bible Extra** ☆ Jeremiah 18:1–6,
2 Timothy 2:1–7, 2 Peter 1:5–9

The acid test

Every leader undertakes seasons of preparation. God tests our faith and takes us through the refining fire. He takes out all that is of human origin and leaves that which has been divinely inspired. Moses spent 40 years in the wilderness. Joseph and David spent 13 years in obscurity. Abraham spent 25 years plus more, in his season of preparation, so that he could fulfil his call to be the "father of many nations". Every skyscraper needs deep foundations and every leader needs them too.

Here are the top 10 tests that God takes leaders through to make them strong and effective.

TOP 10 tests that God takes a leader through (from the life of Abraham)

1. **The familiarity test**
   God asked Abraham to leave his country and his people and go to a land where he'd never been before.

2. **The famine test**
   When Abraham arrived in Canaan the place was in famine. Things often get worse before they get better. Remember – don't run away. Stay committed. It's only the famine test.

3. **The forensic test**
   Abraham lied in telling the details of who his wife was. It's the little foxes that can spoil the vine.

4. **The first-shall-be-last test**
   Abraham told Lot that he could be the first to choose the land that he wanted. Abraham wasn't going to "manufacture" or "force" prophecy to come to pass. God would give the land to him.

5. **The forerunner test**
   Lot was in trouble. Abraham won with only 318 men. God will give you a sample of war and a sample of victory. Be faithful to it.

6. **The first-fruits test**
   What do you do when victory comes? Abraham knew that God had given him the victory. He gave a tithe to Melchizedek to honour God, not himself.

7. **The fidelity test**
   When options are placed in front of you – do you go with Hagar or stick with Sarah? Do you want an Ishmael or an Isaac?

8. **The fruition test**
   It took 25 years for the first part of the promise to come to pass. The time test is often the hardest. Don't quit!

9. **The funeral test**
   God called Abraham to give the dream up – to kill his son, Isaac. Resurrections only come from funerals. The "death of a dream" test is the test of trust and the test of true love. Who would come first?

10. **The finishing test**
    The secret is in the follow-through. Abraham buried Sarah and gave instructions about his son. Many start the race, but fewer finish it. True success is to raise up a successor who will take the baton and run with the promises.

Top 10 ☆ Bible Extra ☆ Hebrews 12:5–13, James 1:2–4, 1 Peter 1:6–9

Make a killing

Followers blame the Devil for too many things. Leaders know that our greatest enemy is ourselves. The Bible says that it's our own "evil desires" that cause the trouble. The only power the Devil has in our lives is the power we give to him through activating the "old man" and giving in to our "evil desires". A man had a dream where he saw the Devil crying in the gutter beside a road. He asked the Devil why he was so sad and the Devil answered "Because people keep blaming me for things I never did". Leadership takes responsibility and ownership of the real problem.

Here are 10 ways to kill the "old man".

TOP 10 ways for leaders to kill the "old man"

1. Suffocation

Jacob said that Judah's hands would be on the neck of his enemies. Judah means "praise". Fill the air with praise and worship and suffocate the "old man".

2. Starvation

The one that wins in the wrestling match between the "old man" and the "new man" is the one you feed the most. Give the "old man" no food and he'll run out of fuel.

3. Conviction

The Holy Spirit convicts us when we are about to activate the "old man". Listen to your conscience and to the guardian of your mind – the peace of God.

4. Redemption

The "old man" is crucified with Christ. God sees you as if you've never sinned. The slate is clean and God's power is more than enough for a life of total victory.

5. Motivation

Increase your vision of God and your God-given future, and your desire to sin will greatly decrease. In the words of the famous song "the things on earth will grow strangely dim, in the light of your glory and grace".

6. Ramification

Do a little thinking about the effect your private life could have upon your public life. That sin could grow into the stuff that ruins marriages and ministries.

7. Restoration

The more you obey, the more God restores – fractures of the soul are healed and the Devil finds it more difficult to tempt you. His foot-holding ability is diminished.

8. Decision

The greatest power you have is the power of decision. Resist the Devil and he'll finally decide to stop annoying you.

9. Magnification

As you magnify the successes of the "new man", you'll create the unsung power of momentum.

10. Repetition

The more you do the right thing, the less you do the wrong thing. The more you create good habits, the more you break bad habits.

Top 10 ☆ Bible Extra ☆ Galatians 2:20, Galatians 5:16–25, 1 Timothy 1:5, James 1:13–15, James 4:6–10

All things work together for good:
"What an excuse to witness to the man at the garage, dear."

Poo happens

The famous bumper sticker is correct – "poo happens" (adapted for Christian readership). The important thing in the life of a leader is to turn that poo into fertiliser. Don't let life hurt you – let it create within you "the roses of success". Proverbs tells us that when there's no oxen in the stall, the stall is clean. Its meaning is clear – whenever you're dealing with people, there's a lot of poo that hits the fan. The leader knows that it's just another opportunity to make all things work together for good and turn that poo into fertiliser that makes us bigger and better than we've ever been.

Here are the top 10 situations that God uses to make us more like Him and be used more mightily by Him.

TOP 10 situations God uses in the making of a leader

1. **Misrepresentation**
   When you're on the cross for something that you never did.

2. **Exasperation**
   When you've done your best and your best just isn't good enough.

3. **Exclusion**
   When someone less experienced is promoted ahead of you.

4. **Submission**
   When you're asked by a leader to do something you just don't want to do (and it's not an issue of unrighteousness).

5. **Desertion**
   When your best friend turns his back on you.

6. **Condemnation**
   When you run with the vision and things go from bad to worse.

7. **Intimidation**
   When you've noticed that other ministries are doing much better than yours.

8. **Insinuation**
   When your intentions are misunderstood and people begin to talk.

9. **Isolation**
   When nobody believes in you.

10. **Dispensation**
    When God challenges you to bless someone who cursed you.

Top 10 ☆ Bible Extra ☆ Romans 8:28,
Philippians 2:5–10, Hebrews 5:7–10

Hearsay

In life there are things that are urgent and important, important but not urgent, urgent but not important and not urgent or important. The combination that is most crucial but most neglected is the stuff that's important but not urgent. Hearing from God on a regular basis is one of those things. Hearing creates faith as well as intimacy. It provides wisdom as well as strategy. It is the leader's best friend.

Here are the top 10 ways that you can hear clearly from God.

TOP 10 ways for a leader to hear clearly from God

1. **Stop looking for a really weird word**
   and start with some general reading of God's word.

2. **Stop being driven by the pressures of life**
   and find a place where you can stop and meditate slowly on the word of God.

3. **Stop looking for just one word from God**
   and start looking for a series of words. God has much He wants to say!

4. **Stop forgetting about all that He has already spoken**
   to you about through preaching, prayer and prophecy. Sometimes He wants to give "progressive" revelation, not brand-new revelation.

5. **Stop living a negative lifestyle**
   that works against creating an environment of faith and intimacy with God.

6. **Stop panicking**
   about not being able to hear from God and start to soak yourself in God's word.

7. **Stop trying to copy someone else's relationship with God**
   and create your own patterns in drawing close to God.

8. **Stop just sitting there and begin to call out to God**
   asking Him to speak into your life and your situation. Ask and it shall be given… seek and you will find.

9. **Stop dismissing the voice of God**
   as just another thought amongst many. Entertain the thought that these thoughts could actually be from God.

10. **Stop trying to go straight into the mysteries of heaven**
    Start by telling God about all of your current needs and ask for wisdom for each of them. Then look for words that are prophetic about your future and the future of others.

Top 10 ☆ Bible Extra ☆ Joshua 1:8–9, 1 Samuel 3:1–19, Romans 10:17, 2 Timothy 1:13–14

Try buying a gym membership:
*"Go for it, Vicar. I've bet the churchwarden £10
you don't make Evensong."*

First things first

They reckon that when chasing tigers in a field of rabbits,
you don't need to be concerned about the rabbits. But,
when you're chasing rabbits in a field of tigers, you really
need to watch out. Life is about priorities. Tigers come
first. A recent best-seller in America is *Don't sweat the
small stuff* by Richard Carlson. It's all about how not to get
exhausted and wound up over stuff that doesn't really
make that much difference. Leaders need to learn to focus
on the right things to allow vision to come to pass.

Here are the top 10 ways on how not to sweat over all of
the small things that can hamper our lives.

TOP 10 ways for a leader not to sweat over small things

1. **Try turning a blind eye**
   to some stuff that you know isn't right. Deal with it another time.

2. **Try keeping the big issues big**
   by always talking them up.

3. **Try to keep working on the wall**
   when the Sanballats of this world try their hardest to get us away from it. Don't be distracted.

4. **Try committing all of your worries to the Lord**
   In creating a request list, you will enter into the promise that the peace of God that passes all understanding will guard your heart and mind.

5. **Try increasing your SQ (spiritual intelligence)**
   by seeking after wisdom and knowledge from the heart of God. Insight releases oversight.

6. **Try developing a system of support**
   where others can be responsible for all of the small stuff so that you can focus on all of the big stuff.

7. **Try buying a gym membership**
   and work off all your frustrations on the Ab-dicator.

8. **Try remembering it's all worth it**
   The small things indicate that something big is happening.

9. **Try knowing only what you need to know.**
   The more you know the more you'll have the urge to fix.

10. **Try developing a sense of humour**
    It's funny how really silly some people can be and how really strange you can be! A good laugh turns mountains back into mole-hills.

Top 10 ☆ Bible Extra ☆ Nehemiah 4:1–5, Nehemiah 6:1–9, Haggai 1:1–11

A devil of a job

Spiritual warfare isn't just about binding the Devil and telling him that he has no right to a particular person or situation. Everything we do in obedience to God is a weapon of spiritual warfare. A leader isn't unaware of the strategies of the Devil and aims to create a lifestyle that pulls down the enemy's plans and drives him out of the way.

Here are the top 10 ways to beat the Devil.

TOP 10 ways for a leader to beat the Devil

1. Realise
that you're the right person, in the right place, at the right time. You're in the centre of God's will. Don't pull back.

2. Realise
that everything you do in obedience to God is a weapon of mass destruction to the enemy's camp.

3. Realise
that the Devil has no right of way into your life unless you give it to him.

4. Realise
that there is a way of escape from every single temptation. Find it and take it.

5. Realise
that you're not called to focus on the Devil or on the circumstance, but on God's ability to break into every situation. Don't "magnify" the Devil.

6. Realise
that those thoughts and pictures in your head are not your own. Stop owning what originated from the Devil.

7. Realise
that in keeping short accounts with God you can prevent handing Satan a licence to gain a bigger foothold in your life.

8. Realise
that the Devil was rendered powerless through the cross and resurrection of our Lord Jesus Christ. Appropriate it.

9. Realise
that God will help you every step of the way. We are always to be power assisted.

10. Realise
that there are some temptations you can avoid. Walk smart.

Top 10 ☆ **Bible Extra** ☆ **Matthew 4:1–11, 1 Corinthians 10:13, 2 Corinthians 10:3–5, Ephesians 4:27, Ephesians 6:10–18, Colossians 2:15, Hebrews 2:14–18**

Snake eyes

Just like the character Christian in John Bunyan's *Pilgrim's Progress*, the journey of leadership is thwarted with many potential pitfalls. Not only are there hazards while attempting to climb the mountains of Godly success, but there are hazards waiting for us even at the summits. More of Everest's climbers die on the way down than on the way up. It's essential always to be alert and watchful.

Here are the top 10 pitfalls of Christian leadership.

TOP 10 pitfalls of Christian leadership

1. **To get our sense of belonging**
    from what we do and not from who we are and the people we "belong" to.

2. **To replace God's ideas with good ideas**
    and move from faith to presumption.

3. **To expand the gap**
    between who we are in private and who we are in public. To preach well but not live well.

4. **To take a little glory for ourselves**
    and move from humility to pride.

5. **To constantly compare yourself**
    with someone else and someone else's ministry; to try to be like them.

6. **To live under the expectations of people**
    and not under the expectations of God.

7. **To put the desire to be popular above the desire to be obedient**
    and choose the easy road.

8. **To stop**
    on the journey of change.

9. **To be deceived**
    by the allure of the world. Beware of the three G's – Girls, Gold and Glory (or the two S's – Sex and Shopping).

10. **To take failure personally**
    and not bury the dead and move on into your destiny.

Top 10 ☆ Bible Extra ☆ Luke 9:23–24, 2 Corinthians 3:18, Ephesians 1, James 2:14–25

Give two hoots (not one)

Generosity is a master key for success in leadership. Joseph gave to the butler and the baker and so became the highest in the land. Jesus gave forgiveness even while on the cross. Barnabas gave of his gift so much so that his real name of Joseph was forgotten for his new name which meant "son of encouragement". The Philippian Church gave financially out of their poverty and so received the promise that God would "supply all of their needs according to His riches in Jesus Christ".

Here are the top 10 ways that a leader can remain generous in spirit and so enter into some amazing promises of God.

TOP 10 ways for a leader to keep a generous spirit

1. **Give praise**
    when someone else's ministry is doing much better than yours.

2. **Give financially**
    when it looks like things are at their lowest point.

3. **Give up standing up**
    for your rights when you know you've been wronged.

4. **Give grace**
    to the people who once supported you but now have deserted you.

5. **Give worship**
    when the best-laid plans lie in ruins.

6. **Give away**
    something that you really really like.

7. **Give without complaining**
    about the cost of the giving. Give thankfully.

8. **Give comfort and strength**
    to others when you're desperate for some comfort and strength yourself.

9. **Give God a big surprise**
    by not asking Him how much you should give to Him. Go beyond the call of duty.

10. **Give wholeheartedly**
    to people and places that have no ability to give anything back to you.

Top 10 ☆ Bible Extra ☆ Proverbs 11:25,
Proverbs 22:9, Matthew 5:40–42, Matthew 6:1–4,
Mark 10:43–45, 2 Corinthians 9:6–15

Keep your hands off:
"But... I'm your wife!"

Indecent proposal

People have affairs for a whole list of reasons. Sometimes they're a way of escape from a difficult time and sometimes they develop out of a desire for extra pleasure in good times. Even the euphoria of success can become a vulnerable time for extra-curricular activity. They come in the guise of romance, mystery, beauty and seduction. They often occur at work. Under the adventure lies the destructive forces of disloyalty and deception.

Here are the top 10 ways for a leader to avoid having an affair.

TOP 10 ways for a leader to avoid having an affair

1. **Keep on the front line**
   David fell not because he was an adulterer, but because he wasn't with the troops when he should have been. Always be on the front line of God's progressive vision for your life.

2. **Keep on the same tracks**
   If you're attracted to someone of the opposite sex, don't go out of your way to foster the relationship. Keep doing what you usually do.

3. **Keep your mind on the job**
   Don't allow your mind to fantasise about anyone you're attracted to. Keep your meditations pure and focused on God's will for your life.

4. **Keep your mouth in check**
   Don't share the details of personal problems between you and your partner with someone of the opposite sex. Don't allow a potential wedge to be placed between you and your ordained relationship. Don't compare your partner to anyone else.

5. **Keep your questions down**
   Don't ask questions about really personal stuff that relates to someone of the opposite sex. You can do without bonding in soul with anyone except your partner, your family and close friends of the same sex.

6. **Keep your company safe**
   Don't be found alone in the private company of someone you're attracted to or even someone you think you could be attracted to.

7. **Keep your hands off**
   If you are giving a hug to say goodbye, make sure that it's short and sweet and you only do it in the company of others.

8. **Keep your eyes from wandering**
   People who like each other often share glances across a room. Make sure that you're not looking for anyone's eyes across the other side of a room. Only have eyes for the right person.

9. **Keep lines of openness**
   If you do find a special attraction that cannot be stopped by points 1–8 above, tell someone and get them to pray for you and work with you in support and wisdom.

10. **Keep your head on**
    Don't exchange your birthright for a fleeting pleasure. Weigh up the consequences of sin. Don't get intoxicated by circumstances or by wine. Always be sober and alert.

Top 10 ☆ Bible Extra ☆ 2 Samuel 11:1–5, Proverbs 6:20–35, Matthew 5:27–30, Philippians 4:8–9, 1 Timothy 5:2

"Freshness is paramount."

Set the world on fire

Most leaders are careful with obvious sin such as stealing and lying. Worldliness is a combination of sins which are far more subtle and can be a destructive driving force in the life of any leader if it remains unchecked. Envy, jealousy, greed and idolatry can manifest themselves in the guise of wanting to succeed, prosper and get ahead in ministry life. It's essential that a leader allows God to search their heart and discover the true motivation behind all they do.

Here are the top 10 symptoms of worldliness in the heart of a leader.

TOP 10 symptoms of worldliness
in the heart of a leader

1. **When the limelight**
   is taken off your ministry and placed on another, you feel hurt and rejected.

2. **When you've lost**
   all gratefulness for what you have today.

3. **When you're always**
   comparing the fruitfulness of your ministry with the fruitfulness of someone else's.

4. **When you ring every man and his dog**
   when things are going great but sit in the shadows when things are not so good.

5. **When you focus**
   on your ministry instead of keeping the focus of your ministry, which is the establishing of God's Kingdom.

6. **When you can't**
   help telling guest speakers to church that this is a low-attendance Sunday.

7. **When you search**
   for compliments every time you do something public.

8. **When you feel**
   driven to buy bigger and better when what you've got is more than sufficient.

9. **When you stretch**
   the truth to gain acceptance and popularity.

10. **When making a good impression**
    and having a good reputation moves to first place on your list of priorities.

Top 10 ☆ **Bible Extra** ☆ Matthew 6:1–8, Acts 8:9–25, Colossians 3:1–17, 1 John 2:15–17

in the

Practical World of
a Christian Leader

"I don't think I have the energy to be a Christian."

Preach up a storm

Preaching is the effective communication of God's word under the influence of the Holy Spirit. Sometimes we spend too much time on the communication side with lots of interesting stories but lack the conviction that causes hearts to be opened and lives to be changed. On the other hand, many have a great thought on their heart and mind but lack the ability to communicate it in bite-size, relatable pieces. The conviction is high but the listeners are few.

Here are the top 10 ways to make and create a great sermon.

TOP 10 ways to prepare a great sermon

1. **What's God been saying to me personally?**
   When you preach, believe that God has chosen you, not Yonggi Cho. There's a good reason for that!

2. **What's God already been saying to the people?**
   Often our preaching looks at the same diamond of truth, but from different angles. It may well be the time for a different angle.

3. **What's the theme of my Christian life?**
   Each of us have a life message. It should come out often when we preach.

4. **What are the building blocks of the Christian life?**
   What are the fundamental truths and principles of the Christian life?

5. **What are the needs of the congregation I'm talking to?**
   Start with the known and move to the unknown. Are they a particular people group? Have they all experienced something together recently?

6. **What guidelines or instructions have I been given?**
   If you're asked to preach on relationships, don't preach on money.

7. **What passages of scripture comes to mind?**
   A certain passage may contain both a theme and some great instruction and principles relevant to the congregation.

8. **What other things might God want to say to the congregation?**
   Ask the Lord and keep an ear to heaven – He may surprise you.

9. **What season is it in the year?**
   Is it a special day or near a special day?

10. **What do I want to say?**
    If you want to say it – you know it'll be fresh. Freshness is paramount.

Korma or curry?

They say that you can tell if someone has the leadership gift by taking them to an Indian restaurant and asking them to decide what to have. Those who decide without questioning the contents can reveal an impetuous nature, while those who take forever can reveal habitual double-mindedness. Making well-thought-through decisions is a leadership trait that needs to be mastered by every leader who desires to excel.

Here are the top 10 ways to make really good decisions.

TOP 10 ways to make really good decisions

1. Try asking "Why?" three times
Get to the bottom of things. What is the real motivation behind the decision being made?

2. Try starting with eternity and working backwards
Eliminate short-sightedness – start with the afterlife and finish with lunch.

3. Try using your brain
Some decisions are much better than others. God has given you a brain to use, not to ignore.

4. Try using the power of the peloton
Learn to cycle with the wise – there is wisdom in a multitude of counsellors.

5. Try staying in the life of faith
Make decisions based on the word of the Lord, not on the amount of money in the bank.

6. Try using the 51/49 principle
Some decisions are just a fraction better than others. There are a number of ways to skin a cat. Decide your way and commit to it 100%.

7. Try keeping an ear to the umpire
Let the peace of God be the umpire and guard of your heart. If your peace blows its whistle, take real notice.

8. Try asking God for wisdom
God will give liberally to all who ask for it. Be open to the unusual word that God sometimes gives.

9. Try trusting in progressive revelation
After you've been faithful to the current word from God, He'll lead you to the horizon where you'll then get the next word from God.

10. Try believing that within you is the mind of Christ
Your thinking is becoming like the thinking of God – stop living under the shadow of doubt.

Top 10 ☆ Bible Extra ☆ 1 Kings 3:4–15, Proverbs 15:22, Matthew 6:19–21, Acts 8:26–40, 1 Corinthians 2:16, Philippians 4:4–7, Hebrews 4:12–13

Krakatoa!

The gifts of the Spirit listed in 1 Corinthians 12 are referred to as the manifestations of the Spirit. Because God lives in heaven and in our hearts, we can receive a gift either down from heaven or up from our hearts. When a volcano erupts, what was under the surface manifests itself for all to see. It's essential that we stir up the gifts that are within us and allow the supernatural to be released from our lives. What an impact we can make!

Here are the top 10 ways to move in the gifts of the Spirit.

TOP 10 ways to move in the gifts of the Spirit

1. **Choose to believe that the same Spirit**
   that rose Christ from the dead now lives in you. You have all that it takes living in you right now.

2. **Choose to believe that it is God's desire**
   that rivers of life flow from your inmost being to touch and impact a needy world. The gifts are manifestations of the Spirit.

3. **Choose to believe that the gifts are grace gifts**
   The Greek word for "gift" actually means "a gift of grace". You don't deserve it. You can't earn it. It's by the grace of God. Stop exalting men who move in the gifts.

4. **Choose to desire the spiritual gifts earnestly**
   Desire is the key that stirs up the gifts and causes them to be released at the point of need.

5. **Choose to step out in faith and not fear failure**
   As you begin to step out, you release the power that accompanies the gifts. You can only learn whether the promptings are from God or yourself by stepping out and "having a go".

6. **Choose to live a life of intimacy with God**
   As you keep regularly "tuned" to the airwaves of God, you'll not miss out on opportunities to move in the gifts of the Spirit.

7. **Choose to hang around people who move in the gifts**
   When Saul hung around the prophets, he prophesied. The right environment can accelerate the rising of the gifts.

8. **Choose to walk in the motivation of love**
   The gifts aren't for show, they are for lifting people to new levels of living.

9. **Choose to allow God to prune you**
   for greater manifestations of the gifts. John 15 tells us that God prunes us for increased fruitfulness. He enlarges our character for greater charisma (the Greek word for gift).

10. **Choose to submit your gifts to the leadership of your church**
    Everything should be done decently and in order. Unruliness can nullify the effectiveness of the gifts.

Top 10 ☆ Bible Extra ☆ Daniel 11:32, John 4:4–26, John 7:38–39, Romans 8:10–11, 1 Corinthians 12:1–11, 1 Corinthians 13:13, 1 Corinthians 14:1, 1 Corinthians 14:26–39

"Dominating Dave can be hard to quieten."

Putting two and two together

Leading small groups can be a real challenge. Dominating Dave can be hard to quieten down while Sensitive Sally needs to put a smile on her face. Pentecostal Pete can be at odds with Newly Saved Nigel and End Times Enid can always be annoying. The aim of the leader is to unite the group that would never have been seen together if it wasn't for Christ.

Here are the top 10 ways to lead a small group.

TOP 10 ways to lead a small group

1. **Try to create a sociable atmosphere**
   When many groups begin a meeting, the atmosphere freezes over. The meeting finishes when someone says "Let's begin".

2. **Try to start with everybody saying something**
   Don't let people slip away into their own world. The satisfaction comes from the affirmation of the participation.

3. **Try to start with thanksgiving and praise**
   Focusing on the victory can be the catalyst for a great night.

4. **Try to avoid prayer times that become morbid times**
   Don't allow melancholy and doubt to infiltrate your times of prayer. Not everything that sounds spiritual has in it the spirit of faith.

5. **Try to quieten the time hoggers**
   Get them on your side with the chance for you both to unite to bring out the more timid members.

6. **Try to stick to the golden rule – no preaching**
   Allow the group to come up with the right conclusions and underline what needs to be emphasised. Preaching can kill the small group dynamic.

7. **Try to encourage the growth of the group**
   Without a progressive vision people soon become inward-looking.

8. **Try to keep it spiritually natural and naturally spiritual**
   The meeting doesn't finish with "Amen", but with the last coffee mug placed in the sink. The meeting didn't start with a song, it started when the first person arrived. A Christian who says "Let's get spiritual" is like a fish saying "Let's get wet".

9. **Try to delegate parts of the meeting to potential leaders**
   To train leaders is a prime role for every leader.

10. **Try to remember that you're not responsible for the members**
    but to the members. Don't strive to make people attend. Ultimately, their Christian walk is their responsibility, not yours. Simply do your best for God.

Top 10 ☆ Bible Extra ☆ Acts 2:42–47, Romans 12:3–8, 1 Corinthians 12:12–31, Ephesians 4:1–7

One thing leads to another

Leadership is the art of taking people from where they're at to a chosen destination. It requires vision, relationship, skill and wisdom. A woman once looked out of a tourist bus in Israel and saw a man pushing and hitting the sheep with a rod to get them to go in a certain direction. She told the tour guide that the behaviour she saw wasn't what she expected from a shepherd. The tour guide retorted "That's not the shepherd, that's the butcher." The art of leading, as opposed to the art of shoving and pushing through guilt and manipulation, is being restored to the Church.

Here are the top 10 ways to excel in the art of leading.

TOP 10 ways to excel in
the art of leading

1. **Create a vision culture**

   Vision isn't a statement, it's a way of seeing. Promote the right people, sing the right songs, pray the right prayers and say the right things. Create a hot-house environment that accelerates vision living.

2. **Create high aerobic strength**

   Out of the heart flows the life of the Church. Create a core team that eats, sleeps, drinks and lives the vision. People don't follow you, they follow the people following you. Look after your heart.

3. **Create anticipation**

   Faith expects results. If not today then tomorrow. If not tomorrow, then the next day. Kill the spirit that kills expectancy.

4. **Create a pace that both challenges and refreshes**

   Pace can make the difference between winning and losing. Know when to deposit and when to withdraw, when to encourage and when to discipline, when to accelerate and when to slow down.

5. **Create a definition of success**

   Success isn't just in the destination, it's in the journey. Success is about attitude and about doing the right thing long enough. Reward what you define as success and you'll get more of it.

6. **Create goals together**

   Set targets together with your leaders. Regularly evaluate progress with goals. Adjust the targets every so often to make them both inspirational and attainable.

7. **Create an excuse-free zone**

   Encourage accountability and responsibility. Create a "yes" culture of willingness and enthusiasm.

8. **Create a rapport that connects you with people**

   Love people more than progress. Put yourself in their shoes. Be both tough and tender, unstoppable and vulnerable. Always see them with the eyes of faith, even when they let you down. Live by example.

9. **Create a God-dependent people**

   Don't be a "superleader". Create people who connect with a super God. Change high-maintenance people into low-maintenance people. Don't just give them fish, teach them how to fish.

10. **Create courses for horses**

    Each person has both strengths and non-strengths. Put the right strengths in the right places and watch them come to life.

Top 10 ☆ Bible Extra ☆ Psalm 23, Proverbs 4:23,
Proverbs 29:18, John 10:1–18, Ephesians 4:7–16

A close call

Leading worship is a mix between worship and leading. You need to be both a worshipper and a leader. Worshippers who don't lead soon lose the people, and leaders who aren't worshippers tend to push the people. Worship leaders don't take people into the presence of God, they begin with the presence of God. During a season of singing a song called "Holy Spirit, let your presence fall", a new Christian came to me with great delight. He said that God was pretty generous with all the gifts He wanted to give us. I asked him to explain and soon realised that he'd been singing "Holy Spirit, let your presents fall". Worship leaders cause people to stand again on the truths of God's word, praise and worship our God and then move into fresh levels of intimacy and revelation.

Here are the top 10 ways to lead worship.

TOP 10 ways to lead worship

1. **Include a good dose of intervention**
   It's time to intervene on behalf of the people and seek the intervention of God. Prayer works wonders and connects you with the people.

2. **Include a good dose of preparation**
   Success is spelt w.o.r.k. The more you prepare the better results it will produce. Spontaneity works well when you know the songs and have the words on the screen.

3. **Include a good dose of declaration**
   Don't begin by crying out to God – begin by declaring the great things that He has done. Hallowed be Thy name!

4. **Include a good dose of anticipation**
   Anything can happen when God is lifted up. Usher in an atmosphere of expectation. When anticipation fades, it's time to stop.

5. **Include a good dose of transaction**
   Make your leadership a two-way affair. Get people to lift up their hearts, voices and hands. Encourage them to receive blessings from heaven.

6. **Include a good dose of construction**
   Hymn sandwiches are only bad if they're stale. A song list that's well constructed with praise leading to worship creates a clear path into the heart of God.

7. **Include a good dose of instruction**
   Tell them what's going on. Encourage the people to walk the journey into the praise and into worship.

8. **Include a good dose of exaltation**
   Let God be exalted. Let eyes be taken off their past and their limitations and fixed upon the Lord of heaven and earth.

9. **Include a good dose of perception**
   Know when to leave a song for the next. Know when to enthuse and when to be quiet. Know what the Spirit is saying.

10. **Include a good dose of relaxation**
    After you've done the above nine points, relax. It's not by might or power, it's by the Spirit of the Lord.

Top 10 ☆ Bible Extra ☆ Psalm 95:6–7, Proverbs 20:4, Isaiah 61:3, John 4:24, Romans 12:1

Complicated reports encourage nit-picking:
*"If we cut down on our cat food expenditure,
we might see fewer mice."*

Clash of the titans

Every Church needs an AGM – the
infamous Annual General Meeting.
It's often a meeting where cracks
are prized open, doubts are aired
and votes are cast. The key to
everything, including AGMs, is
great leadership.

Here are the top 10 ways to have a
successful (and enjoyable) AGM.

TOP 10 ways to have a successful AGM

1. **Make sure that you have created a one-heart leadership team**
   Out of the heart of the church flow the issues of life. Good issues come from good hearts.

2. **Make sure that you fill the room with praise**
   for everyone who is partnered in the vision. Without them – it would all remain a dream.

3. **Make sure that you fill the room with praise reports**
   from people who always have a good report.

4. **Make sure that you give some commendation**
   for some of the people who have made sacrifices way beyond the call of duty.

5. **Make sure that the financial overview is done last and not first**
   Jesus made Judas the treasurer to get him away from the most important issue – the people. Vision precedes provision.

6. **Make sure that your attitude is always that the glass is half full**
   Don't despise the day of small beginnings or magnify the opposition.

7. **Make sure that you relate your journey**
   of realising your vision to a prophetic example or prophetic word from scripture.

8. **Make sure that you always present the vision**
   as being in the middle of construction. You've come so far, but the best is yet to come. Then encourage greater participation and commitment.

9. **Make sure that the finances are presented**
   in an easy-to-read format. Give just enough to satisfy. Complicated reports encourage nit-picking.

10. **Make sure that you know that it's God who has called you**
    and not a committee.

Top 10 ☆ Bible Extra ☆ Numbers 13:26–33,
Proverbs 4:23, Zechariah 4:6–10, Ephesians 6:7

Community chest

Jesus said that the harvest was plentiful. The word "plenty" means not just a few and not the whole lot. It's simply more than expected. In your city, town and village people are hungering after God. There are not just a few, it's not everyone, but it's more than you'd expect. Starting a community centre is just one way to connect the church with the harvest.

Here are the top 10 things to watch for when starting a community centre.

TOP 10 things to watch for when starting a community centre

1. **Never talk about the church and the community centre**
   as being two different things – the community centre is the church in action.

2. **Never value people according to their wealth or standing**
   Create a centre for every type of person and see each one as equally valued.

3. **Never just create courses**
   create pathways. Running a slimmers' club is great, but unless it leads to a "searchers' club" we can miss the harvest.

4. **Never allow the "glamorous" ministries to take precedent**
   Everyone has a heart for the orphans, prostitutes and homeless. They provoke imagination. Most people, though, don't fall into these extreme categories. Church should start with the general before going to the extreme.

5. **Never let the church cool down**
   in it's love for the lost. The more you are actively involved in the practical lives of people, the more you can forget that their real need is salvation.

6. **Never let the church think that they don't have to reach out**
   any more because the community centre is doing it for them. Ninety-five per cent of people are added to the church through relationships, not projects.

7. **Never go for short-term results**
   Community centres are about salting whole communities with the love of Christ. Credibility costs thousands of pounds and thousands of hours.

8. **Never allow political correctness**
   to get a stronghold in management. Positive discrimination can be as unfair as negative discrimination. Everybody is equal.

9. **Never allow the pedantic people to take the leadership**
   There are a lot of issues to be worked through in every centre, but leadership should remain in the hands of visionary, strategic and positive people.

10. **Never take money that could jeopardise your future**
    Unrealistic goals associated with the granting of money can lead to either the side-tracking of ministry or a replacement of leadership.

Top 10 ☆ Bible Extra ☆ Isaiah 61:4, Matthew 25:31–46, Matthew 28:19–20, Acts 1:8, James 1:27

On a wing and a prayer

Prayer is often seen as something you've got to do but not something to enjoy doing. The "legalists" enforce it every time they speak. If it becomes a chore, it loses its potency. It's the prayer of faith and the prayer of desire that connects well with the heart of God and sees answers returned.

Here are the top 10 ways to make a prayer meeting a really great place to be.

TOP 10 ways to make a
prayer meeting a great place to be

1. **Change the packaging**
   "Divine encounters night", "master asker night", "command and conquer night" are all better names for a meeting than "night of prayer".

2. **Change the way you start**
   Start with a word of inspiration that raises the expectancy – "we can make history tonight".

3. **Change the time limit**
   It's always better to create a short prayer meeting that goes over time than create a really long prayer meeting that drags on and on.

4. **Change the pace**
   Have times of declaration, times for small groups, times for corporate prayer and times for worship. Like a great movie – pace is essential.

5. **Change the confidence level**
   Reinforce the fact that our confidence is in the fact that He hears us. If He hears us, He'll answer us.

6. **Change the emphasis**
   Each prayer meeting will have some different emphasis inspired by the Holy Spirit.

7. **Change the leadership**
   Use it as an opportunity to exercise the leadership gifts of up-and-coming leaders. It may add to the freshness factor.

8. **Change the flow**
   Don't allow it to be led by those with the loudest voices or most dominant spirits.

9. **Change the mood**
   If it starts to get melancholic, lift the spirits and reinspire with praise and worship. Some mistake navel-gazing for waiting in the presence.

10. **Change the language**
    Don't fake hunger. You can't hunger after God if you're not hungry. Ask God to increase your hunger for Him. Keep the language authentic.

Top 10 ☆ Bible Extra ☆ 2 Chronicles 7:14,
Mark 11:23–24, Ephesians 6:18, 1 John 4:14–15

The wow factor

Church services can be really boring and uninviting. Our culture is looking for things that captivate, inspire and stir the soul, and that should only be the beginning of all we do. Often people leave the spirit of excellence in their workplace and treat the services of a church as a leftover at the end of the week. Our church services are the shop window of church life, the rally point of church life and the big celebration of all that Christ has done, is doing and will do in our lives and in our nation. Surely, it's time for excellence.

Here are the top 10 ways to make a church service a great experience.

TOP 10 ways to make a church service a great experience

1. **Take Mr Grumpy off door duty**
   and replace him with Mrs Enthusiasm.

2. **Take away the quietness that's mistaken for deep spirituality**
   Liven it up with the sound of laughter and anticipation.

3. **Take away the pressure to have to attend church**
   Tell them that if they don't want to be there, go home.

4. **Take Miss Boring off the announcements**
   Stop making God's weekly will so uninteresting.

5. **Take away the supermarket own-brand coffee**
   and buy something a little more expensive.

6. **Take away really deep preaching**
   Install the kiss rule – keep it simple, stupid!

7. **Take away the music stands**
   and let the musicians and singers spearhead the way of excellence by memorising the words and the music. Encourage them to look like they're enjoying themselves!

8. **Take Mr Wannabenoticed off the flag-waving**
   and put him on the tea-making.

9. **Take away the long-winded preaching**
   Buy a timer with a buzzer.

10. **Take away the sacred cows**
    such as Mrs Doyley's crocheted tablecloths and replace with a fresh and appealing environment.

Young blood

Youth ministry is tough at the best of times. Often the youth leaders are still working through a lot of stuff in their own lives and they're given the entire responsibility for a whole lot of other lives. There's not much praise from the youth and definitely a lot less from the parents. There's pressure from the elders because the youth don't sit still in church and if that's not enough, the Devil is somewhere around as well.

Here are the top 10 things you definitely need to know about youth ministry.

TOP 10 things you definitely need to know about youth ministry

1. **Youth ministry is passion personified**
   It's the heart of enthusiasm for every church. Let their passion drive the music, fuel the worship, fill the testimonies and impregnate the atmosphere. Take the "suits" off the front rows and let the youth sit there.

2. **Youth ministry is "pay per view"**
   It is payment by instalments. Teenagers don't just make one big decision for Jesus but a series of mini-decisions. Each decision lets them view that bit more of God's amazing call for their lives.

3. **Youth ministry is a time-saving device**
   Prevention is better than cure. The smart money is in an awesome youth programme that puts teens on the right footing for life. It saves lots of time of "adult" ministry.

4. **Youth ministry is the most volatile**
   They go from the top of Everest to the depths of the earth in a day. Trust that under all the emotion is a faith that will keep them from falling.

5. **Youth ministry is prone to the pack instinct**
   They arrive in a pack and leave in a pack. Within the pack, though, are lone wolves hungry for God.

6. **Youth ministry is about pushing the limits**
   Safe is boring. Outrageous is more like it.

7. **Youth ministry is a matter of being "wise as serpents"**
   In attempting to be relatable, the youth leader sometimes takes on the same spirit as the people he's trying to help.

8. **Youth ministry is a prophetic ministry**
   If you change the youth, you can change the nation. Almost every movement for good or for bad has been through a youth revolution.

9. **Youth ministry is not a stepping stone**
   Full stop.

10. **Youth ministry is much more than youth ministry**
    It's also ministry to the parents, crowd control, health and safety supervision, damage limitation, child protection, financial assistance and family planning.

The transfer market

How do you make a dream become a reality? How do you get people to catch your vision so entirely that it becomes their vision? How do you transfer your passion so that it affects every-one that you're targetting?

Here are the top 10 ways to get people to see the vision the way you see it and rally together to see the dream come to pass.

TOP 10 ways to get everyone to catch the vision of a leader

1. **Release the vision creators**
   Leaders create vision. Give yourself permission to be inspired by God and create a vision that becomes irrepressible and irrefutable. Stop living under people's limitations.

2. **Release the vision collaborators**
   Find other leaders who are called to be mentors, modellers, fathers and friends. Share your vision with them and release the power of collaboration. Let them visit and share their passion.

3. **Release the vision casters**
   Leaders cast the vision. Create opportunities for casting the vision through preaching, publicity and prayer.

4. **Release the vision clarifiers**
   There are leaders and there are managers. Managers clarify how the vision will work. They find solutions and strategise.

5. **Release the vision connectors**
   Some people are born to sell. They're the people people, who love to be the life of the party. Search them out and empower them to connect people with vision, people with people and people with leaders.

6. **Release the vision carriers**
   Vision is often caught, not taught. The carriers spread the vision by rubbing shoulders with people. They let people browse before buying.

7. **Release the vision converts**
   There are some people who are already the first fruits of what all your dream is about. Promote their testimony and release their spirit.

8. **Release the vision custodians**
   There is always the next generation that needs to run with the dream. Select future leaders who will one day take the baton for you. Teach and train them in the things of God.

9. **Release the vision clusters**
   Break the vision into smaller parts and raise up people to work in teams for the success of the vision. Departmental teams, area teams, service teams... teams of all shapes and sizes where the vision can infiltrate into the lives of every person.

10. **Release the vision catalysts**
    Getting started in a small way can cause a momentum that creates a snowball effect. Provision starts to flow and signs and wonders follow. Momentum is the hidden force of every successful ministry.

A dream ticket

Teamwork is brilliant when you've got a team that works. To create a team that works, begin by looking at the selection process for people to be part of the team.

Here are the top 10 things to look for in creating a dream team.

TOP 10 things to look for in creating a dream team

1. **Choose someone who is not fully grown**
   Always choose people who are still growing into their God-given potential. If they're not teachable, don't choose them.

2. **Choose someone who accepts the "family values"**
   Every team leader has some particular ways of doing things. Select people who respect those ways and aren't always trying to change them.

3. **Choose someone who is not a volunteer**
   Volunteers need constant praise and upkeep. A team needs people who join out of a sense of calling. Their reward and encouragement then comes from God. The team can be advancement-focused and not maintenance-minded.

4. **Choose someone who is not standing on a stepping stone**
   Choose people who will work with all of their heart. People who use one team to get to another, only work with half a heart. They are half-hearted. You can do better than that.

5. **Choose someone who brings a good report**
   Teams need people of faith. Twelve spies went out but only two were rewarded because they had a good report. Don't accept cynicism and doubt.

6. **Choose someone who is willing to pay the cost**
   God sets fire to altars. Find people who are willing to put themselves on the altar of sacrifices. It attracts the power of God.

7. **Choose someone who is transparent**
   Don't use someone you can't really get to know. God builds teams on relationship, not just function. Don't employ scarlet pimpernels!

8. **Choose someone who supports the team from the bench**
   Select people who are passionate about scoring, not about who scores. Look for people whose security isn't wrapped up in position.

9. **Choose someone who speaks the same language**
   Every team has a lingo – a way of speaking indicates a way of thinking. Unity is the uniting of thought for a common goal.

10. **Choose someone who has the right gifts and talents**
    Select people on the basis of both character and gifting. Skills can be learnt but gifts and talents are inherent. Search for it.

Top 10 ☆ Bible Extra ☆ Exodus 18:15–26, Numbers 11:14–17, Numbers 14:5–9, 1 Samuel 14:1–15, 1 Timothy 3:1–13

TOP
10
OF EVERYTHING

in the

Handy Hints World of
a Christian Leader

Their glazed eyes gave the game away:
*"Died last week, right – but tell me, did the Lord
speak to you during my sermon?"*

Have an ear-full

Being a good listener isn't easy. Many
leaders live in "overload" and even
though they try hard to listen, their
glazed eyes give it all away.

Here are the top 10 ways to be really
rude when you're talking to someone.

TOP 10 ways to be really rude when you're talking to someone

1. **Regularly look behind them**
   at all the other people you'd like to be talking with.

2. **Regularly say "that's good"**
   even when they tell you about their looming bankruptcy.

3. **Regularly say you'll pray for them during the week**
   and then forget all about it.

4. **Regularly forget their name**
   and ask them for the twentieth time to remind you what it is.

5. **Regularly butt in**
   and tell them you've been through some worse times.

6. **Regularly bring someone else into the conversation**
   who is passing by, then suddenly make a break for it.

7. **Regularly share some confidential information**
   about other people and tell them to keep it confidential.

8. **Regularly ask them about their kids**
   when they don't have any.

9. **Regularly have bad breath**
   and stand really close to the other person.

10. **Regularly look like you're home**
    but the lights aren't on.

Help!

Sometimes we think that abnormal is normal and normal is exceptional. It's time to get more confident with what you believe the normal Christian experience should be all about. What kind of Christian are you looking to develop and what kind of church do you think gives the best opportunity for Christians to grow into champions of the faith? Here are a few people that we've all met (and been) and some solutions to help them on their journey to maturity.

Here are the top 10 types of Christians who really need your help.

TOP 10 types of Christians who really need your help

1. **Striving Stanley**
   Stanley is never happy and always frowning. He always wrestles with condemnation and never thinks he prays enough. Solution – affirmation and encouragement that he's doing great!

2. **Mystic Meagan**
   Meagan is always looking for heavenly signs. She always has a couple of visions each day and loves "end times" teaching. Solution – get her into the children's ministry where rubber always meets the road.

3. **Demonic Daniel**
   Daniel sees demons behind everything. He even thinks that if he could just get that one more demon out of Stanley, he would be really free. Solution – tell him to be less nosey and only ask him about the good things God is doing.

4. **Counsellor Colin**
   Colin loves to use all of the counselling course material on any willing participant. He often has a perceptive and slightly aloof air about him. Solution – get him in the evangelism team and back to reality.

5. **Whatever Wendy**
   Wendy is so laid back she's almost asleep. Nothing phases her and she wonders what all the fuss is about. Solution – extra hours at work and a crisis to stir the soul.

6. **Hypocritical Harry**
   Harry loves to look really great on Sundays and he's always dressed smartly. His video collection at home gives a completely different picture. Solution – an altar call.

7. **Impetuous Ian**
   Ian always says "yes" to everyone. He runs at 100 mph and then crashes. He comes and goes like a yo-yo. Solution – a good talking to and the passing of time.

8. **Spirit-led Sarah**
   Sarah only comes to church when the spirit leads. She's a part of the city-wide church and meets in a mid-week intercessory group. Solution – avoid her – it's all a mask for rebellion and independence.

9. **Simple Simon**
   Simon believes everything and is quickly cornered by Counsellor Colin and Demonic Daniel. He even borrowed some videos from Hypocritical Harry. Solution – a good cell group with good role models.

10. **Cynical Cynthia**
    Cynthia has been burnt in the past and not moved on. She loves crossing her arms and thinks everything is one big act. Solution – keep preaching faith. Don't look at her when you're speaking publicly. It will only discourage you.

Excuse me

Some Christians have mastered the art of trying to escape responsibility. It's all dressed up in spiritual clothing and all done decently and in order. It's hilarious.

Have a look at the top 10 ways for Christians to escape responsibility. Make sure you're involved in none of them!

TOP 10 ways for Christians to escape responsibility

1. **Tell them**
   you'll pray about it.

2. **Tell them**
   you've been led by the spirit to another ministry.

3. **Tell them**
   that you felt the Lord say that you needed "time out".

4. **Tell them**
   that you just don't feel that your gifts lie in that particular field.

5. **Tell them**
   that your ministry is more prophetic than practical.

6. **Tell them**
   that you'll do it when you feel God move you.

7. **Tell them**
   that your time is taken up in intercession.

8. **Tell them**
   that you think you're coming to the end of a season and you're not sure what the new season is yet.

9. **Tell them**
   nothing – just don't turn up and avoid the subject if asked about it.

10. **Tell them**
    that you're leaving the church. They're all a bunch of hypocrites!

Top 10 ☆ **Bible Extra** ☆ Matthew 25:1–30,
Acts 2:42–47, Philippians 2:1–16, James 1:22–25

Counting the congregation creatively.

Up for the count

One of the most frustrating things about leadership is how slow it is to get your ministry to grow. God gives the increase but sometimes we lose patience waiting for it.

Here are the top 10 ways to speed it up by doing some creative accountancy. They are the top 10 ways to count your congregation, or group, or department.

TOP 10 ways to count
your congregation

1. **Install turnstiles**
   and make sure that the toilets are on the opposite side of the turnstile from the meeting hall.

2. **Include all the pregnant women**
   Count them as two.

3. **Include all the people who didn't come**
   but call the church their home.

4. **Introduce three people to count the congregation**
   Always pick the highest figure.

5. **Involve your evangelist in the role of counting**
   The figure is sure to be higher than normal.

6. **Insist on always counting "in faith"**
   Surely the numbers will be higher than when counting with the natural eye!

7. **Invite the whole community to come**
   and tell them that you're giving free shopping vouchers from a major supermarket to all who turn up. Then count.

8. **Indulge in complete denial**
   and keep preaching to thousands.

9. **Introduce a mirror wall on the side of the worship hall**
   and then get someone visually challenged to count.

10. **Interview for the job of counting**
    and only select teenagers who use excessive words such as "mega" and "awesome".

Have the last laugh

Having a sense of humour is a must for the backpack of every leader.

Here are the top 10 ways not to take yourself too seriously.

TOP 10 ways not to take
yourself too seriously

1. **Get someone**
   to do an impersonation of you and join in the laughter with every-one else.

2. **Get a group**
   of people to quote you some of your "faux pas" and laugh hilari-ously.

3. **Get chuckling**
   about some of the people who have left your church.

4. **Get relaxed**
   and find a Lazarus, Mary and Martha. Use their house as a place of rest and relaxation.

5. **Get out of the habit**
   of dividing fun times and spiritual times. Have spiritually fun times!

6. **Get a realisation**
   that a great failure was the proof of a great attempt – celebrate!

7. **Get to grips**
   with the fact that the whole thing is beyond you. It was designed to be. That's your life!

8. **Get sharing**
   in your sermons about some of the stuff you really enjoy that you know is a bit quirky. Let them see a bit more of the real you.

9. **Get a life**
   outside of the life of ministry. Have fun with unsaved people.

10. **Get out more**
   and see that you're doing better than you think you are!

Avoid sharing something about your loved one.

Avoid like the plague

Being a good speaker isn't just about having something to say or about saying it in a really interesting way that leaves people both inspired and challenged. It's also about not allowing little things to distract from the main points that you're trying to make.

Here are the top 10 things to avoid when speaking publicly.

TOP 10 things to avoid when speaking publicly

1. **Avoid using a list of examples from the "Book of Illustrations"**
   Personal stories are always the best.

2. **Avoid using exaggerations**
   Be enthusiastic but stay truthful. How many were actually saved at that African mission?

3. **Avoid taking pot-shots at your antagonists**
   Don't preach at people – preach to them.

4. **Avoid swearing**
   Apart from the obvious, watch out for culture differences in the meaning of some words.

5. **Avoid too much repetition**
   Stand up. Speak up. Shut up.

6. **Avoid using the expressions "Hallelujah"**
   and "Praise the Lord" to fill in the blanks while you think of what to say next. Religious jargon is a putter-offer.

7. **Avoid sharing stuff over which you haven't got the victory**
   Testimony is what you get when you've succeeded at the test.

8. **Avoid sharing something about your loved one**
   that they just didn't want revealing.

9. **Avoid the peacock walk**
   two steps forward, two steps back. Try standing on the same spot, even when excited!

10. **Avoid all other funny mannerisms**
    Ask the youth to imitate you and you'll notice the stuff you do that's distracting from the message.

Happy as Larry

There are some things that really excite leaders. Sometimes we're taken by surprise!

Here are the top 10 things that bring back that buzz factor and make ministry all the more enjoyable.

TOP 10 things that really excite a leader

1. **When you ask someone to do something**
   and you find that they've already done it.

2. **When you have to tell people to stop giving**
   because you've met your target.

3. **When you correct someone**
   and they immediately respond with a positive attitude.

4. **When someone not only hears the preaching**
   but does it.

5. **When you find out someone's given up**
   their annual holidays in order to help fund the vision.

6. **When someone had a great idea and then did it**
   No more procrastination.

7. **When someone who's a whiz on guitar in the church band**
   spends their after-service times loving people without the guitar anywhere in sight.

8. **When you invest a lot of time on a "wild card"**
   and they become a champion.

9. **When someone wins someone who wins someone to Jesus**
   It's the makings of revival.

10. **When someone doesn't give the leader the benefit of the doubt**
    They just never doubted.

Mad as a hatter

Here's my chance to let off some steam. What gets leaders really mad is that they can't often show it. People punch you, abuse you and say all kinds of nasty things about you and the only thing you can do in return is smile. Leaders need to take care. It's the retaliator not the initiator that gets the red card in football and it's the same with leadership. It's so unfair!

Here are the top 10 things that get leaders really angry.

TOP 10 things that really make a leader angry

1. **People who**
   say that they're right behind you then suddenly disappear. (You really want people right beside you, not right behind you.)

2. **People who**
   say that we need more prayer and then fail to turn up when you put on that extra prayer meeting.

3. **People who**
   say that we'll need a bigger building soon, then slip out the back door when the fundraising begins.

4. **People who**
   think that they've got that extra edge in spiritual revelation.

5. **People who**
   gather a little following and call it a ministry.

6. **People who**
   just sit there after the meeting is finished.

7. **People whose**
   first letter to you is a letter of complaint, not a letter of praise.

8. **People who**
   always wear their heart on their sleeve.

9. **People who**
   everyone thinks are wonderful, but the leader knows the truth.

10. **People who**
    tell you that you're looking tired and need a holiday, then do nothing to lighten the load (or sponsor a holiday!).

Putting the house in order

Sometimes people can be really out of order. We are always giving people the benefit of the doubt but deep in our hearts we know that, each week, those prophecies and long-winded prayers are simply a call to be noticed. It's not really "spiritual" at all. It's time we stopped the interruptions to the service and brought in some simple guidelines on how things are going to work from now on. That's leadership!

Here are the top 10 ways to stop someone constantly interrupting a really good service.

TOP 10 ways to stop someone constantly interrupting a service

1. **Get them on car parking duty**

2. **Get them to stop prophesying for a season**
   until we've been able to process the last 26 prophecies.

3. **Get praying that God would open their eyes**
   to see the love of God and to know who they really are in Christ.

4. **Get your leaders praying out loud and prophesying**
   so much that there's no time left for anyone else.

5. **Get a simple list of new guidelines**
   that state how the service will run in the future and why.

6. **Get some ear muffs**
   when they tell you that you are "quenching the spirit".

7. **Get some partnership going**
   and tell them to hold fire in order to encourage others to step out.

8. **Get a little heart-test going**
   and tell them that if they have a "word", write it down and give it to you afterwards.

9. **Get them to see**
   that, possibly, their ministry lies elsewhere.

10. **Get someone to become their friend**
    and start to minister to their real needs.

Top 10 ☆ Bible Extra ☆ 1 Corinthians 14:26–40,
2 Timothy 2:25–26, 2 Timothy 4:1–5

Waffle-maker

Every preacher waffles at times, but some more than others. Waffling is never seen by the preacher as waffle. It is seen as an important addition providing revelation and insight to the lives of those listening.

Here are the top 10 ways to waffle when preaching!

TOP 10 ways to waffle when you're preaching

1. **Say**

   that you don't know why you said what you said and imply that it must have been the Spirit.

2. **Say**

   "finally" and then make sure that you give at least another four "finally"s.

3. **Say**

   only what you could prepare in between dinner and *Match of the Day*.

4. **Say**

   everything you dislike – your pet hates, your grievances and your thorns in the flesh.

5. **Say**

   everything you heard recently from somebody else's sermon without properly thinking it through.

6. **Say**

   things about up-and-coming world events and how they are all directly linked to certain scriptures. Say sorry in three years' time.

7. **Say**

   so much about the historical references that you avoid all practical references.

8. **Say**

   so many interesting stories that you forget why you started telling them in the first place.

9. **Say**

   things that make you sound much more intelligent than you actually are.

10. **Say**

    that you're going to do another part of the 48-part series you started the year before last.

Bon voyage

Escaping from the ministry is a thought that's crossed the mind of every Christian leader.

Here are the top 10 ways to escape from ministry and leave all your troubles behind!

TOP 10 ways to escape from ministry

1. **Buy a second house on the Canary Islands**
   and call it "Bethseda Gospel Hill". Have regular missions trips.

2. **Buy a gym membership**
   and spend three hours a day there. Call it evangelism.

3. **Buy a good spy book**
   that has nothing to do with deep spiritual truths.

4. **Buy your team huge presents**
   and encourage them to work harder. The more they work, the less you need to!

5. **Buy all the stuff for that hobby**
   you should have started seventeen-and-a-half years ago.

6. **Buy a stamp and post a letter to yourself**
   saying that you deserve an extended holiday for being such an awesome, inspired, first-class leader.

7. **Buy some space in the local paper**
   and advertise your services as Administration Whizz, Child Carer Expert, Motivational Guru, Conflict Manager, Greeter par Excellence and Odd Jobs Specialist.

8. **Buy a season ticket**
   to the Bahamas.

9. **Buy a paper**
   and, if you're on church staff, look for all of the other jobs you could be doing. Apply secretly.

10. **Buy two theatre tickets for you and your spouse**
    and try not to talk about the ministry for the entire night.

Removing team spirit.

Goodbye sweetheart

Team spirit is an important part of team building. People will line up to be part of a team that has a great spirit. Heart and soul play a huge role in the eventual success of my team. Technical brilliance is only part of the story.

Here are the top 10 ways to zap team spirit!

TOP 10 ways to remove team spirit

1. **Tell them**
   that you're always there for them and then when they call you up, tell them you're too busy to talk.

2. **Tell them**
   that even though they've done their best, it's still not good enough.

3. **Tell them**
   that you really believe in them and then when one's left the room, pull them down in front of all the others.

4. **Tell them**
   that they've got a week to do the job, then spend each day looking over their shoulder until it's done.

5. **Tell them**
   that things aren't up to expectation without ever giving them a list of expectations.

6. **Tell them**
   stories about how great other teams are and subtly make them feel inadequate!

7. **Tell them**
   that unless they rise up you're going to sack them.

8. **Tell them**
   nothing at all after they've had some massive successes.

9. **Tell them**
   all about your new car with the CD changer just after you've cut their spending budget.

10. **Tell them**
    how it's an honour for them to be working for you.

TOP 10 OF EVERYTHING

in the

Wide World of Knowledge of
a Christian Leader

Behind closed doors

Leaders are always on the look out for doors of God-given opportunity. They are either passing through doors or pressing against doors. Many people simply hang around doors in a world of procrastination and indecision. There are 10 doors of opportunity that God wants us to see, open and pass through, leading to greater effectiveness and fruitfulness in our lives and the lives of all that we influence.

Here are the top 10 doors of God-given opportunities.

TOP 10 doors of God-given opportunities

1. **Invisible doors**
   After Paul went to Troas, he noticed that God had opened a door and he'd gone through it (2 Corinthians 2). Automatic sliding doors of God open when they sense that we're coming through.

2. **Open doors**
   Paul stayed on in Ephesus – a "great door for effective work" had opened up to him. If the door opens – go through it (1 Corinthians 16).

3. **Open doors no man can shut**
   Psalm 24 talks about opening the "ancient doors" so that the king of glory may come in. Your connection with heaven is an open door that no man can shut. His "covenant of peace" will never be removed.

4. **Closed doors that some can open**
   In Luke 11, the man who was sleeping at midnight said to the man who begged for food for his friend, "Don't bother me, the door is already locked...". Because of the boldness of the one who begged, the door was opened. Prayer can be the key that opens the door.

5. **Locked doors that no man can open**
   In Matthew 25, the five virgins found the door shut to the banquet hall and their request for entry rejected. These are doors of lost opportunity.

6. **Doors of hope**
   Hosea 2 states that God will make the "valley of Achor a door of hope". Achor means trouble. In every valley of trouble and turmoil is a door of hope that leads to a place of great advancement.

7. **Doors of intimacy**
   In Revelation 3, Jesus tells us that He stands at the door and knocks. If anyone opens the door, He will come in and dine with them. It's the door of intimacy.

8. **Doors of insight**
   In Revelation 4, John noticed a door standing open in heaven. It led him to the balcony of insight where he could see what was about to take place. God has wisdom and understanding for those who desire it.

9. **Door of sacrifice**
   In Luke 13, Jesus says to make every effort to enter by the narrow door. Resurrection life always comes out of real surrender.

10. **Doors of confession**
    The Psalmist asks the Lord to "keep watch over the door of my lips" (Psalms 141). Proverbs tells us that life and death are in the power of the tongue (Proverbs 18). Your confession can become an instant door of God-given opportunity.

Top 10 ☆ Bible Extra ☆ Matthew 25:14–30

Go by leader-ship

Miracles never happen in the shallows. Faith living is always deep-water living. When every exit door is shut, God comes into His own. Christian leadership is not by human might or power, but championed by the Spirit of the Lord. After you've heard from God, pushed out into the deep, dropped your nets for a catch (after catching nothing all night), you find yourself in a perfect position to see the "super" come back into the natural. Don't stay on the shore. Let your leadership come out of the harbour and be touched by the power of heaven.

Here are the top 10 ways leaders can work by leader-ship and put the "super" back into natural!

TOP 10 ways a leader can put the "super" back into natural
(from the story of the woman and the jars in 2 Kings 4:1–7)

1. **Always find yourself in an impossible situation**
   She had no ability to pay her debts. Her son's freedom was in jeopardy. If you're in leadership, this first point is easy-peasy.

2. **Always know that our God is a sovereign God**
   She was not just any widow – she was the widow of one of the prophets with Elisha. More goes on behind the scenes than in front of them.

3. **Always have a desperate heart**
   She cried out to the prophet. Beggars can be choosers. Leaders are master askers.

4. **Always wait for the prophet's instruction**
   She was asked to collect pots. Find the word of the Lord for each situation – no matter how crazy.

5. **Always give what you have**
   She had nothing… "except"!

6. **Always plant seeds for a coming harvest**
   You reap what you sow. According to her pots, be it unto her. The oil stopped flowing when the pots stopped coming.

7. **Always shut the door behind you**
   She created a faith environment. Shut the door to doubt and negativity.

8. **Always expect great things from God**
   As she poured, the oil multiplied. As you step out in faith, the miraculous begins – never beforehand.

9. **Always anticipate the Lord's continued blessing**
   She asked for another jar even though they found none left. The oil would have kept flowing if the vessels had kept appearing.

10. **Always return for further instructions**
    She came back to the prophet and he gave her further instructions. Seek God's word at Ai as much as you did at Jericho. His ways are higher than yours.

Top 10 ☆ Bible Extra ☆ Luke 5:1–11, 2 Kings 3:1, Zechariah 4:6

To make mistakes is our birthright:
"But I only said that Father Christmas didn't exist!"

Like it or lump it

There are many things that a leader must learn to accept. In our pursuit of destiny, we all prefer to take the shortest route at the fastest speed. Wisdom has decided that our destiny won't rest in the destination but in the journey taken. Sometimes the details demand patience and our patience leads to perfecting. Even though we plan our course, the Lord determines our steps. Some mountains are to be removed, others are to be climbed. Some rivers are to be avoided, others swum. Some things are to be rejected and other things accepted.

Here are the top 10 things all leaders need to accept.

TOP 10 things that a leader needs to accept

1. **To please everyone is to attempt the impossible**
   You will never please everyone all of the time. You'll always have at least one enemy. You can, though, fully please God.

2. **To make mistakes is our birthright**
   Failure is often the sign of a great attempt. Successes are never gained without failures.

3. **To feel limited, under-prepared and ill-equipped is normal**
   God always takes leaders beyond where they're at so that they walk by faith and trust and eventually all the glory goes to the ultimate leader – Jesus Christ.

4. **To get to a new level of authority and anointing requires steps, not elevators**
   We plan our course, but God determines our steps. Great oaks start from little acorns. We want to go from A to C. God wants us to go from A to B to C.

5. **To experience the reversals of God is par for the course**
   If step A is bearing fruit and step C is bearing more fruit, then step B has something to do with pruning.

6. **To be disappointed is to be unexpectantly expected**
   A leader expects great things all of the time. Part of the package then is to quickly and regularly brush off disappointments and then expect again with the eyes of faith. If not today, then tomorrow.

7. **To have a bumpy ride is natural**
   Every new programme and every new leader has a honeymoon period. It's not a problem when the rubber hits the road – it's normal.

8. **To be faithful in small things is the pathway to promotion**
   Be encouraged, then forget this point. It may distract you from being faithful to today because you're always looking to tomorrow. The journey of 1000 miles starts with one step. (Don't despise it.)

9. **To say "whatever will be will be" is right (after all is said and done)**
   Faith is associated with action – and trust is associated with surrender. After you've done all you can and kept the faith – what will be will be.

10. **To be big is not always to be beautiful**
    You can be a flash in the pan and a one-hit wonder. To build correctly and to create a team of leaders takes time but eventually proves to be the wisest way. The tortoise often wins over the hare.

Top 10 ☆ Bible Extra ☆ James 1:1–5, Colossians 1:10–12, Proverbs 16:9, Psalm 37:23, John 15:1–2

Make it big

Every leader wants growth. We want all that we do to expand, multiply and accomplish great things for Jesus. Sometimes growth happens much slower than we ever anticipated. It's only for some future vantage point that we realise that growth has occurred. We need to be smart though. There's a difference between muscle and fat but under clothing it can look much the same. We want to build the church and not just a crowd.

Here are the top 10 types of growth that ministries can have.

TOP 10 types of growth that a ministry can have

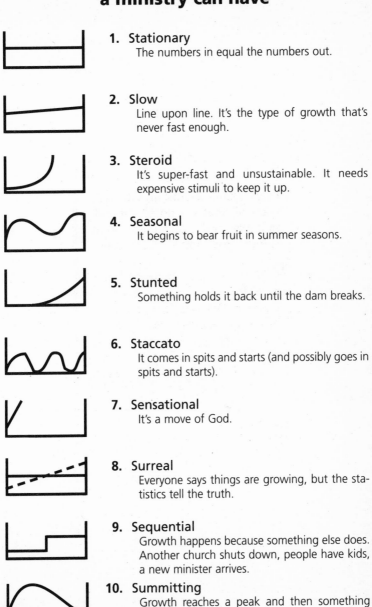

1. **Stationary**
   The numbers in equal the numbers out.

2. **Slow**
   Line upon line. It's the type of growth that's never fast enough.

3. **Steroid**
   It's super-fast and unsustainable. It needs expensive stimuli to keep it up.

4. **Seasonal**
   It begins to bear fruit in summer seasons.

5. **Stunted**
   Something holds it back until the dam breaks.

6. **Staccato**
   It comes in spits and starts (and possibly goes in spits and starts).

7. **Sensational**
   It's a move of God.

8. **Surreal**
   Everyone says things are growing, but the statistics tell the truth.

9. **Sequential**
   Growth happens because something else does. Another church shuts down, people have kids, a new minister arrives.

10. **Summitting**
    Growth reaches a peak and then something causes a decline.

Troubled waters

God will always take people out of their depth in order to keep them living by faith and cause their capacity to increase and gifts to emerge. Leaders, however, often take people too far beyond their level of faith and gifting, causing people to eventually quit under the strain and pressure.

Here are the top 10 reasons why we promote people to incompetence and often never see them again.

TOP 10 reasons why we promote people to incompetence

1. **We notice that someone has excelled**
   in a particular ministry and we want to reward them with a more "important" position.

2. **We put gifting above character**
   and then watch the person crack under the new pressures of responsibility.

3. **We put character above gifting**
   and place a person in a role which is way out of their league. They just can't do it.

4. **We fall into the extrapolation trap**
   We think that people can continue to expand and excel at the rate they've been displaying. It's unsustainable. Expansion is followed by consolidation, not expansion.

5. **We think that "the sky's the limit"**
   We think that everyone has the same potential if they only believed it. God, however, gives us a measure of faith and a measure of gifting.

6. **We feel intimidated and pushed**
   into giving certain people more noticeable roles.

7. **We get flattered by the compliments and gifts**
   of certain people and unwisely promote them.

8. **We promote people who have no proven record**
   of faithfulness and trustworthiness.

9. **We give jobs for the boys**
   even if our friends are unequipped and ill-prepared.

10. **We try to reignite someone's fire by giving them a promotion**
    instead of instilling in them a progressive vision for what they're already doing.

Top 10 ☆ Bible Extra ☆ Luke 16:1–12, Acts 6:3–4, Romans 12:3–8, 1 Corinthians 4:2

Snap!

We all think that the grass is greener on the other side of the fence. People are the same everywhere and, despite the publicity, most good churches and ministries go through similar experiences as you because they all involve people.

Here are the top 10 truths about the growth of any church.

TOP 10 truths about
the growth of any church

1. **In a growing church**
   the numbers coming in the front door are one more than the numbers going out the back door.

2. **In a growing church**
   the number of people away on any given Sunday is over 20%.

3. **In a growing church**
   the number of people who leave always looks more than the number of people arriving.

4. **In a growing church**
   the number one enemy isn't the attitude of those who leave but the attitude of those who continue to attend but remain unchanged.

5. **In a growing church**
   the number of people who regularly attend church isn't the same as the number of people who are the church. Within the crowd is the congregation.

6. **In a growing church**
   the number of people present may stay the same, but they're not all the same people. Each year, 15% of people will have been released and replaced.

7. **In a growing church**
   the number of people who fall on the path, live in shallow soil and grow amongst thorns will never be zero. Jesus prophesied it.

8. **In a growing church**
   the number of people who make up the good seed in good soil will one day bring forth exponential growth. Jesus prophesied it.

9. **In a growing church**
   the number of seasons a church goes through will always be four – spring, summer, autumn, winter.

10. **In a growing church**
    the number of new people coming to church are a part of one of three categories – seed planters (saved in the house), pot plants (drawn to the house) and house plants (transferred from house to house).

Uncommon sense

One of the great friends of a leader is common sense. We so often look for the mystical and look to the unusual that we miss the obvious.

Here are 10 questions with only one very obvious answer.

TOP 10 questions with only one answer

1. How do you grow a church without confrontation?

2. How do you grow a church without wanting to?

3. How do you grow a church with minimum effort?

4. How do you grow a church that's boring?

5. How do you grow a church without expectations?

6. How do you grow a church without risk?

7. How do you grow a church without leadership?

8. How do you grow a church without first-time visitors?

9. How do you grow a church without losing people?

10. How do you grow a church with everyone voting "yes"?

Consumers, not producers:
"Not a guitar in sight!"

Breaking up is hard to do

Gloria Gaynor once sang the words "never can say good-bye". One of the hardest times for a leader is when people leave. There's not one reason why people leave, there are many. Often in church life, the people God uses to take the vision of the church from A to B will be different to the people he uses to take it from B to C. Some of that is God's doing and some is man's doing. Sometimes it may feel that people are leaving us, but the truth is that we leave them when they choose to go no further into the heart of God's purposes. People come and people go but God remains the same and remains committed to all His promises.

Here are the top 10 reasons why people leave your church.

TOP 10 reasons why people leave your church

1. **They never arrive**
    They are with you in body but not with you in spirit. Their heart remains elsewhere. Some hearts are caught in the memory of the past, others trapped in being in love with the world.

2. **They are only called for a season**
    Some people are called to a particular church for a season. They give their heart and soul, and then are propelled to unite with another ministry. Often they are sent but many just leave.

3. **They decide to go no further**
    When the train leaves the station, some decide that this is as far as they are going. They decide to live in "Haran" and not head for "Canaan". Some people are brought to the end of the bridge they never burnt and then return from whence they came.

4. **They decide that they can't win**
    Some people think that if they stay they can change the way things are run. Often when the place begins to grow, they send in their letter of resignation. Their influence is marginalised and they know it. The reason they give for leaving is rarely the real reason.

5. **They never deal with the offence made to them**
    They get offended and the offence leads to bitterness. The offence is never forgiven nor the situation resolved.

6. **They never receive the help that they need**
    If the congregation fails to stir up their gifts and fails to step out in love and faith, people will fall off the edge. If expectations are given but not met, disillusionment will lead to distancing.

7. **They never correct their motivation**
    Some want position and promotion. They look for a platform of recognition that gives them a sense of value. When the position is given to another, they leave.

8. **They are consumers, not producers**
    Some treat church like a restaurant. After tasting the food on offer they head for other buffets with new taste sensations. They head for the next best thing.

9. **They are beyond the capacity of the church**
    Every church has a growth capacity that's limited by the capacity of leadership. Some leaderships cannot accommodate the additional growth and some additional growth has a higher capacity than the existing leadership.

10. **They are removed by God**
    Some people who continue to grieve the Spirit and antagonise the flow of the Spirit are removed by the Spirit. They often say that they're led elsewhere, but it's not the case.

Top 10 ☆ Bible Extra ☆ Matthew 13:18–23,
Matthew 19:16–24, John 6:53–70, Acts 5:1–11, 2 Peter 1:5–9

God's game plan

What does the 21st-century church look like? What kind of church does God want his leaders to create? The church is God's plan A and God's plan B. He's chosen the church to bring about the transformation of our world. It won't happen despite the church, but through the church. It is the leader's greatest aim to champion the cause of the local church.

Here are the top 10 characteristics of a 21st-century church.

TOP 10 characteristics of a 21st-century church

1. **A church that is vision led, not just commitment led**
   It's a church that is mobilised by the power of vision, creating a climax of excellence and extravagance.

2. **A church that is built on discipleship and not attendance**
   It's not the number of people attending that makes up the church, it's the number of people who are being transformed by the Spirit of the Lord.

3. **A church that is built on a pattern of sound teaching**
   No more lurching from fad to fad. It's a church that lives and breathes the principles of New Testament teaching and one that weaves on the fabric of truth into the lives of believers.

4. **A church that does the right thing long enough**
   Sheer persistence and longevity produces the breakthroughs of God. It's a church that doesn't just dabble, it commits.

5. **A church that comes under Apostolic power**
   The church is built on the foundation of the Apostles and Prophets. The 21st-century church is influenced and impacted by the leadership of the Apostles of the faith in connection with the Prophets of the Spirit.

6. **A church that is led by strong, effective leadership**
   Strong, clear and wise leadership creates a church that is unified and empowered to get results.

7. **A church whose capacity is always expanding**
   The greater the capacity of the leadership, the greater the ministry of the church. The greater the capacity of the church, the more it grows.

8. **A church with a clear path from community to core**
   People need a clear path into the central life of a church. Weak areas of ministry can thwart the journey of people moving from the outskirts to the "inskirts" of church life.

9. **A church that has more than a belief system**
   The 21st-century church doesn't just believe, it steps out with mountain-moving faith. It walks the talk.

10. **A church that creates a sense of belonging**
    People need to belong. They need to partner in the vision. The 21st-century church values and mobilises its ministers through networks of small groups and teams.

Top 10 ☆ Bible Extra ☆ Matthew 16:18, Ephesians 2:20, 2 Timothy 1:13, Hebrews 6:12, 1 Peter 2:4–10

Believe it or not

Faith is an inner con-
fidence that God will
do what He said He'd
do. Every leader is
called to walk by
faith and not by
sight. Faith sees the
future as God sees it
and propels us to
take a hold of it with
both hands.

Here are the top 10
things to know about
walking in faith.

TOP 10 things to know about walking in faith

1. **You can't just make it up**
   It comes from an original word from God. Either you get it or you don't. You can't just half-believe.

2. **You can't get it through the laying on of hands**
   It's not transferable. You can't borrow faith. You can live in an atmosphere of faith yet still have no faith.

3. **You can't avoid reality and live by faith**
   Faith confronts the situation and then overrides it with a higher truth. Faith speaks to the mountain, it doesn't avoid it.

4. **You can't have faith without it being tested**
   God wants to take the wishful thinking out of your faith. Pure faith the size of a mustard seed can do incredible things.

5. **You can't confuse faith with activity**
   Faith is a noun. It is a state of being. It is so confident that it wants to push out into the deep for a catch. Make sure that your activity is filled with faith and your faith is filled with activity.

6. **You can't help but see the miraculous when you've got faith**
   Positive thinking finds the one chance in a hundred that something can be done. Faith finds there's no chance, yet launches out and sees awesome, "supernatural" results.

7. **You can't throw the baby out with the bath water**
   Just because some have abused the teachings on faith, this does not eliminate faith from being the only currency heaven deals with.

8. **You can't just confess something and see it happen**
   Your confession must be accompanied by real believing, renewed thinking and restored living.

9. **You can't please God without it**
   Faith must be the foundation of our holiness, our pursuits, our ministry and our future. It's not an added extra for the optimists.

10. **You can't have faith and at the same time sweat profusely**
   By faith we enter into rest. Take a break from striving – have a holiday!

Top 10 ☆ Bible Extra ☆ Romans 1:17, Romans 5:1–2, Romans 10:17, Hebrews 11:1–39, 1 Peter 1:6–9

Ouch!

Conflict management is an art that every leader needs to develop. There will always be someone in conflict with the vision, the values, the expectations and the procedures of every minister and every church. There will always be clashes over personality, and issues of justice and righteousness. How the leader handles the friction will determine much of the outcome of their future.

Here are the top 10 ways to handle conflict in the ministry.

TOP 10 ways to handle conflict in ministry

1. **Be committed to the truth**
   that all things work together for good, eventually. Increased capacity and team strength are born out of conflict.

2. **Be committed to understanding the real reasons for conflict**
   Often the issue discussed is not the real issue at hand. Unresolved issues can masquerade under current non-issues.

3. **Be committed to staying out of the boxing ring**
   Don't get into a fight. Don't make life complicated for yourself.

4. **Be committed to getting wisdom from God**
   Strategies from heaven range from leaving it alone and giving it to prayer through to hands-on involvement. Know when to compromise and when to tackle head-on.

5. **Be committed to the destiny of the people in conflict**
   Always include the big picture of believing in their God-given future. Dowse the conflict in faith and destroy negativity and fatalism.

6. **Be committed to keeping to the one agenda**
   If an issue has been raised, never bring up unrelated, historical issues that can only complicate matters.

7. **Be committed to humility**
   Be the first to apologise even if you're 99% justified. Let your attitude to the 1% create a "grace" culture that breaks down resistances.

8. **Be committed to knowing that He's the God of justice**
   Don't waste time trying to justify what's right or trying to vindicate your name when things go sour. God justifies and resurrects truth, even when it's buried six feet under.

9. **Be committed to getting outside support**
   We all need mentors and advisors as well as people onto whom to cast our cares. Don't carry it alone. Go to God and go to others.

10. **Be committed to your future**
    Mistakes and failings must be placed on the learning curve and then buried in the past. God doesn't expect perfection yet.

Top 10 ☆ Bible Extra ☆ 1 Kings 3:7–9, Psalm 37, Proverbs 15:1

A bird's-eye view

Vision is defined as the ability to see the future as God sees. Visionary leaders both see and declare their God-given future before it arrives and then create the steps to bring it to pass.

Here are the top 10 benefits of being a visionary leader.

TOP 10 benefits of being a visionary leader

1. **Vision is the best motivator**
   To show someone a picture of divine possibility is to inspire them to action.

2. **Vision takes people beyond the call of duty**
   It causes people to focus all of this energy onto a God-given dream. It destroys the enemy called "average".

3. **Vision produces consistency**
   When the going gets tough, the tough turn back to the vision. They choose to see through their inner eyes.

4. **Vision unites**
   Amos says "How can two walk together unless they be agreed?" Vision brings agreement.

5. **Vision attracts provision**
   Provision arrives after the vision commences.

6. **Vision stops small things becoming big**
   Vision keeps the main thing the main thing. Molehills remain as molehills.

7. **Vision creates creativity**
   Where there's a will, there's a way.

8. **Vision rejects alternatives**
   It says "no" to substitutes and tributaries.

9. **Vision removes di-vision**
   Vision exposes people who live by a different vision. It separates one from the other.

10. **Vision taps the eternal**
    Vision exists where there are no tangible possibilities. It brings heaven to earth and swallows the temporal with the eternal.

Top 10 ☆ Bible Extra ☆ Joshua 6:2, Judges 6:11–16, 1 Samuel 17:34–37, 2 Kings 6:17

"Every harvest is miraculous."

Sow what

It's the mission of every leader to move people from wilderness living into Canaan living. The wilderness represents a place of just enough while Canaan represents a place of more than enough. In the wilderness they simply gathered their daily food while in Canaan they reaped according to what they had sown. The wilderness represents the childhood stage of Christianity while Canaan represents the adult stage of taking personal responsibility for the outcome of both provision and victory.

Here are the top 10 principles of sowing and reaping.

TOP 10 principles
of sowing and reaping

1. **Every harvest needs a seed**
   Every Goliath needs a stone and every Red Sea needs a rod. If there's no seed, there's no harvest.

2. **Every harvest is determined by the size of the seed**
   Sow sparingly and you'll reap sparingly. A big harvest requires a big supply of seed.

3. **Every harvest is never instant**
   It never appears before the seed is sown. Faith plus action then waiting for God's reaction.

4. **Every harvest needs good soil**
   The environment you live in will help determine whether the seed will remain dormant or multiply abundantly.

5. **Every harvest requires a harvester**
   Not all of life is seed time. At some stage it moves from prophecy to fulfilment. Don't miss the season to reap.

6. **Every harvest is miraculous**
   Mark 4 tells us that the harvest grows mysteriously while the farmer is both awake and asleep. It is God's harvest.

7. **Every harvest results in thanksgiving**
   God makes sure that the harvest is brought in through faith so that it might come by grace and result in great praise to God.

8. **Every harvest needs the best seed**
   God won't accept just any old seed. The first of the harvest is what God adores, but the leftovers He despises.

9. **Every harvest is determined by the type of seed**
   If you sow your seed into the harvest fields of the unsaved, you'll reap souls for the Kingdom. If you sow in friendliness, you'll reap friendliness. If you sow in hatred, you'll reap hatred. Whatsoever a man sows – he reaps.

10. **Every harvest is a certainty**
    If you've sowed in faith, don't give up. The darkest point is just before the dawn. Confess and believe, wait and trust.

Top 10 ☆ Bible Extra ☆ Ecclesiastes 11:1–6,
Mark 4:26–27, 2 Corinthians 9:6–11, Galatians 6:7–10,

All enquiries regarding this publication and Dave Gilpin's speaking engagements to be made to:

V3 leadership
The Megacentre
Sheffield
S2 5BQ
United Kingdom

Tel: +44 (0)114 272 5077
email: info@v3leadership.com
www.v3leadership.com

Information and resources can be found at
www.hopecity.co.uk